LIFE AFTER LUST

A Journey *Beyond* the Sex Industry

Trixie Racer

TRIXIE RACER

Copyright © 2023 by Renewed Mind Publishing House
Las Vegas, Nevada
Printed in the United States of America.

All rights reserved. No part of this book may be used or reproduced in any form whatsoever without prior written permission of the Publisher except in the case of brief quotations in critical articles or reviews.

Library of Congress Cataloging-in-Publication Data
Renewed Mind Publishing House
Life After Lust: A journey beyond the sex industry.
ISBN - Paperback: 979-8-9882994-0-0
ISBN - Hardcover: 979-8-9882994-2-4
ISBM - Audiobook, 979-8-9882994-3-1
ISBN – eBook: 979-8-9882994-1-7
    1. Self-care, Health. 2. Psychology

Neither the publisher nor the author is engaged in rendering professional advice to the reader and shall not be liable for any loss or damages allegedly arising from information or suggestions within this book. This book is for entertainment and not meant as a substitute for seeking professional medical or mental help. Names and details have been changed. No part of this book is meant to identify any specific living person.

www.lifeafterlustbook.com

TABLE OF CONTENTS

ACKNOWLEDGEMENTS
INTRODUCTION
Chapter 1 - A NEW BEGINNING
Chapter 2 – CHILDHOOD CATALYST
- Attachment styles

Chapter 3 – STIGMA
- The effects of stigma on individuals leaving the sex industry
- The importance of addressing and overcoming stigma

Chapter 4 – GUILT, SHAME, AND SELF-BLAME
- Internalized stigma
- Overcoming self-blame, guilt, & challenging negative self-talk
- Focusing on strengths and accomplishments
- Healthy boundaries

Chapter 5 – SUPPORT SYSTEMS
- Building a support system: Establishing connections for a healthy transition

Chapter 6 – INTIMATE RELATIONSHIPS
- New partner who already knows about your sex worker past
- A new partner who did not know about your sex worker past
- How to tell a new partner about your past
- How to disclose your permanent STI to a new partner

Chapter 7 – TOXIC OTHERS
- You've been outed
- Stalkers
- Types of digital real-time stalking and how to protect yourself
- Pimps

Chapter 8 – CAREER
- Exploring new paths and possibilities
- The resume

Chapter 9 – FINANCIAL TRANSITION
- How to budget
- Credit

Chapter 10 – BALANCE
- Work-life balance
- Relationships
- Making new friends
- Self-care
- Integrating work, relationships, and self-care

Chapter 11 – LEGAL
- Expungement and arrest relief
- Moving on
- Family law

Chapter 12 – PHYSICAL AND MENTAL HEALTH
- Nutrition
- Eating disorders
- How to know if you are a good weight
- Needing a psychiatrist
- Can I regulate with vitamins?

Chapter 13 – SOBRIETY

Chapter 14 – FOR THE PARENTS
- If your children's friends find out
- Your child(ren) inappropriately exposed

Chapter 15 – TRAUMA
- Trauma-specific therapies

Chapter 16 – SEXUAL AFTER-EFFECTS
- BDSM
- Littles/Middles
- Sex addiction
- Sex as self-injury
- SASI is not sex addiction

Chapter 17 – CORE BELIEFS
- Differing religious values
- Spirituality & personal values: Rediscovering your core beliefs
- Identifying misaligned beliefs

Chapter 18 – CONCLUSION

ABOUT THE AUTHOR
RESOURCES LIST

ACKNOWLEGEMENTS

Trixie Racer is not my real name. I quit the adult industry almost a decade ago and abandoned my online blog and social media accounts some years later. So, while I have not identified as Trixie Racer in years, I put that name on this book to demonstrate that I am indeed someone who worked within the sex industry.

I authored this book to help those exiting the industry deal with their leftover residual baggage which does not disappear after quitting. Throughout my own journey, I had to learn most of this on my own. Thankfully, I found many excellent people who made a dramatic difference in my life. To them, I have immense gratitude.

This book became possible due to caring professionals who helped me along my healing journey: Rawan Shrum (The Justice Project), Gabi Smith (Community Coalition Against Human Trafficking), Nia Baker (independent therapist), Jo Velasquez (psychologist), and Melinda Keesy (independent therapist).

Thank you to my closest personal friends who faithfully provided unconditional support and showed me love while knowing my darkest secrets: Ana Sancho Pereira, Steven Crow, Danny Paris, Juan Jose Acuña Leandro, and Marian Vargas. I also want to thank my child for enthusiastically encouraging and cheering me on as I wrote my first book (without knowing the content). And lastly, I want to thank Grandpa Tom for being the most stable platonic male support that I've ever had. You shaped me and made my ability to succeed possible. I love you all.

INTRODUCTION

Sex work, adult industry, sex industry. Throughout this book, I am going to use these terms interchangeably to be inclusive of anyone who has worked in a field that could potentially cause orgasm for the client. This includes strippers, massage therapists, dominatrixes, sex workers, providers, prostitutes, escorts, sugar babies, and porn actors. Whether orgasms occurred due to lapdancing, the other person masturbating, a happy ending massage, oral sex, sexual intercourse, or part of a sexual performance show, sex work is the label I am assigning here. This is not meant to offend you. I blanket label like this for the simplicity of drafting this book, acknowledging that these occupations do differ, yet all of them can find communal value, help, and healing within these pages.

Leaving the sex industry can be a difficult and overwhelming process. It often requires starting from scratch and rebuilding your life from the ground up. You are not alone on this journey. Millions of people, myself included, have gone through it and came out the other side with a new sense of self and purpose. This book will help you. It is possible to discover your worth and build a fulfilling life outside of the sex industry in the mainstream world without feeling permanently damaged.

The purpose of this book is to build your boundaries and self-esteem and provide you with guidance, support, and resources to help you through your transition. We will explore topics such as self-compassion, healing from trauma, addiction, rebuilding your self-worth, healthy vs. toxic relationships, legal considerations, and developing new skills and career paths. There is a lot here. This book will not be perfect and cannot possibly cover everything, but it is a great starting place and will hopefully uncover and point you in the correct direction for anything else that you need additional help with.

People enter sex work for all sorts of reasons, some by choice and some not. Hopefully, you are reading this book because it is your decision to quit. You want a guide who has been through this already to hold your hand and prepare you for what to expect. Not to seem dramatic, yet it is a fact that quitting sex work will affect your entire life, and the aftermath may last for years. You will likely have mixed emotions with relief, fear, doubt, and uncertainty all mingling together as you make changes. With this guide, you will be able to rebuild yourself at a faster pace. Whether you are quitting due to age, injury, mental health reasons, social pressure, school or work, fleeing from being trafficked, or simply because you feel it is time for a change, know that you are taking a brave step towards creating a new life for yourself.

Throughout this book, we will work together to explore your values, goals, and dreams for the future. You are encouraged to take a compassionate and non-judgmental approach to yourself as you navigate this process. There is a strong emphasis on stigma and building up your self-esteem because these are some of the more difficult aspects of quitting and can affect you long-term. You will notice that there is a lot of repetition because many concepts throughout the book (addiction, self-compassion, and trauma being just a few examples) are highly related.

Every human being possesses an innate worth, a value that transcends the circumstances of our lives. After leaving the sex industry, the journey to rediscover and reclaim your intrinsic value might seem particularly challenging. When you find yourself in situations where your self-worth is undermined, you can be left feeling vulnerable and unsure of your own potential. This book seeks to help you navigate the complexities of starting anew and building a life that celebrates and honors your inherent worth.

It is important to recognize that transitioning to a new life will not be easy. Old patterns, habits, and beliefs often prove to be difficult to break. However, this journey is not only about leaving your past behind but also about embracing a newfound sense of self-worth and happiness. You will cultivate self-compassion, a vital ingredient in rediscovering your worth and healing from past experiences.

Some of you who are reading this believe that you are broken; others believe they made it out unscathed. I used to fit both since I tricked myself into believing I was fine, while simultaneously ignoring my self-harming behavior as if it wasn't related. If you ever self-harm, you are not fine. You may not know why yet, but you will. Once you identify your reasons for self-harming, you can stop and learn to genuinely love yourself. That is what healing looks like.

In the chapters that follow, we will explore numerous aspects of rebuilding your life after leaving the sex industry. Just a short sampling of the topics we will cover are:

- Overcoming stigma: Learn how to navigate and confront the social stigma that often attaches itself to the sex industry and advocate for yourself in the face of prejudice.
- Emotional healing: Discover strategies for coping with the emotional challenges and how to develop a powerful sense of self-worth.
- Building a support system: Understand the importance of surrounding yourself with positive influences and learn how to establish a network of supportive friends, family, and professionals.
- Career opportunities and education: Investigate new career paths and educational opportunities that can help you achieve financial independence and a sense of purpose.
- Physical and mental health: Uncover ways to prioritize your physical and mental well-being, including when to seek professional help and setting up new healthy routines.
- Cultivating self-compassion: Learn how to practice self-compassion and self-kindness as a means to

nurture your emotional growth and resilience.

As you work through this book, remember that everyone's journey is unique. There is no "single right way" to move forward after leaving the sex industry. However, there are many wrong ways. Try not to get stuck. There are steps that can speed you along, and those will be covered. By cultivating self-compassion, seeking support, and striving for growth, you will rediscover your inherent worth and then can embrace a life that truly reflects your values, dreams, and potential. You are not defined by your past. You are worthy of love, respect, and a fulfilling life. Let this book be your guide as you embark on the path towards self-discovery, healing, and a brighter future.

CHAPTER 1
A New Beginning

Transitioning from the sex industry to the mainstream world is a momentous change, and even more so for those of you who have only ever done sex work. While each person will have their own novel experience, there are aspects of the mainstream world that may surprise you. Some will be noticeable immediately; other things could take years to notice and work through. Through this book, I am here to forewarn you so you know what to expect and will offer guidance and support to help you navigate these changes. This first chapter will give you a taste of what the transition is like, and then the book will continue to expand on much of what is briefly touched on here. You can always return later to this first chapter as a brief motivational talk. It is not too deep, and it is a good quick review.

First, even after you have left the sex industry, you will probably continue to face stigma or discrimination based on your past work experiences. This can complicate your employment search or ability to form healthy new social connections. People who know might treat you differently than they would have otherwise. If you are single, you may automatically be judged as an easy conquest by people you consider dating. Prepare yourself for potential challenges and develop strategies for addressing these issues. Get a therapist whether you feel like you need one or not. Actively seek out resources, support groups, career counselors, job training programs, and build your support network to help alleviate some of the difficulties associated with sex work stigma and discrimination.

Adjusting to different work dynamics might be tougher

than you expected, and you could be surprised at just how different things are. The mainstream work environment has extremely different expectations, rules, and dynamics than the sex industry. You will find that you will now have to deal with a more structured work schedule, hierarchical management, and team-based collaboration. Be patient with yourself and others, and understand it will take time to learn, adjust to, and adapt to new workplace norms. When you want to quit your mainstream job, I recommend that you first ask for the opinions of 3 people whom you trust that have not worked in the adult industry. They will be the voice of reason when you lack it. This is because you may want to throw in the towel and go back to what you already know; that is common—but not your current goal, which is evidenced by you reading this book.

As you transition to the mainstream world, you will encounter legal and financial responsibilities, taxes, insurance, and employment contracts. If these are new for you, navigating them can be complex. To minimize your stress during the first year, seek out advice or assistance from professionals with experience in these areas. Developing personal financial management skills, budgeting, and learning how to save will be crucial skills for ensuring your long-term financial stability.

You can expect to feel a range of emotions, relief, sadness, excitement, fear, or anxiety, about the future as you leave the sex industry. This is normal. Acknowledge your feelings and communicate with friends, family, and mental health professionals as needed for support. Whether you lean on your partner will depend a lot upon the dynamic of your relationship because many sex workers have been openly or covertly pimped. Do not assume that you have not been until after you read the section on pimps. Engaging in self-care activities, exercise, meditation, therapy, massage, and pursuing personal interests will help you to adjust to the emotional and psychological rollercoaster.

Entering the mainstream world means forming new personal and professional relationships and building a new support network. You will create new connections with colleagues, although you should be aware that the normal oversharing that occurs within the adult industry can be dangerous and put your job at risk within the normal world. So, while it is good to be friendly at work, your new job is not the best place to make new close friends. To widen your friend circle, find extracurricular activities that you enjoy, research events that spark your passion, become a gym rat, or go to a social club. Websites such as Eventbrite.com list events happening everywhere in the United States, even for semi-rural areas. Being open to new experiences and actively seeking opportunities that will expand your social circle outside of work is vital.

You may find that you need to learn new skills, pursue further education or training, or adapt your existing abilities within the context of new industries in order to transition into the mainstream workforce. Dedicate some time and effort toward researching your desired industry, identify transferable skills, and create a plan to get you there. This is a time for personal and professional development. It should be both exciting and challenging.

As you transition, you will eventually come to reevaluate your own self-concept and personal values. It is likely that you developed a persona or false identity specific to your work in the sex industry. Similar to the need to be single for a while in order to recenter and learn who you really are before moving on after a serious relationship break-up, leaving the adult industry will also require some buffer time of self-reflection and personal growth activities. Identify who you are now, what your core values are and whether you have been respecting them, and who you want to be in the future.

It is crucial that you prioritize your personal safety and well-being during and after the transition. When we are busy or overwhelmed, self-care is often what gets neglected, and it is essential that you do not fall into that trap. Good mental health will support everything else in your life, so be aware if you are having mental health difficulties and actively seek help. If you left a dangerous situation, remain cognizant of that at all times and be cautious of what you say and who you trust. Seek resources for physical and mental health care, develop a safety plan for dealing with potential threats, and build a support network of trusted individuals who can help you in times of need.

This is a personal journey and will require your ongoing commitment and support. Be patient with yourself, seek help whenever needed, and maintain a positive attitude while navigating the unique challenges and opportunities that come with this change. By being proactive in addressing potential difficulties and staying focused on your goals, you can successfully transition into the mainstream world and create a fulfilling life outside the sex industry. This is the plan.

As you continue your journey away from the sex industry and into the mainstream world, it is normal to meet moments of doubt or uncertainty. This is when you should remind yourself of your strengths, resilience, and accomplishments. Recognize that it is normal to have ups and downs because this is a process. Hopefully, you are not alone and have a healthy support network. If you do, make sure you stay connected with as much of this healthy support as you have access to, which might include family, friends, mentors, and mental health professionals. These relationships can supply guidance, encouragement, and understanding. Nurture these connections, as they will be a valuable source of strength and reassurance during your transition. However, even if you do not have that type of support and are currently alone, there are organizations which truly do care about your well-being and are there to help you succeed in your transition. Do not allow yourself to be completely isolated.

Personal growth is an ongoing process, and self-discovery is a lifelong journey. You will learn more about yourself, your values, and your desires as you adapt to your new environment. Embrace your authentic self by reminding yourself that you have unique qualities and are a valuable person. Develop a powerful sense of self-worth and self-compassion. Recognize your accomplishments and learn from your experiences.

A sign of growth is permitting yourself to be vulnerable by expressing your desires, fears, and emotions with yourself and (after you feel healed enough to do so) with others. Authentic communication deepens relationships and creates stronger bonds. Focus on and appreciate the positive aspects of your life, both big and small, and maintain an optimistic outlook to stay grounded during times of change. Make gratitude part of your lifestyle.

Set realistic goals and expectations for yourself by creating achievable milestone steps and then celebrate your progress to sustain motivation and remain focused on your long-term objectives. Understand that setbacks may occur, so treat them as learning experiences and opportunities for growth. Reach out to your support network to seek guidance from those who have experienced similar situations. Set aside time to reflect on your journey and the progress you have already made. Each of your accomplishments is another step forward and a testament to your strength and resilience.

Cultivate a healthy lifestyle by taking care of your physical health through regular exercise, a balanced diet, and sufficient sleep. This cannot be overstated. To help you process emotions and keep a positive mindset, pay attention to your mental and emotional well-being through incorporating practices like mindfulness, meditation, or journaling. You do possess the strength and resilience to overcome challenges. Trust in yourself, your abilities, and know that you deserve happiness, success, and a supportive community. Therapists and support groups can assist you with valuable insight and suggest coping strategies for dealing with emotions. Remember: seeking help is a sign of strength and self-care.

Explore your interests and passions by taking part in meaningful and fulfilling activities. These pursuits will contribute to your sense of identity and purpose outside of the sex industry while also leading to new friendships and building your support network. Consider volunteering or offering support to others going through similar transitions. Sharing your insight might empower both yourself and others.

Do not be afraid of stepping out of your comfort zone and trying new experiences. Mainstream life may seem boring at first, yet challenging yourself to experience it fully can lead to personal growth and help you discover new interests, skills, and passions. Embrace the idea of lifelong learning and be open to expanding your knowledge and experience. You are not just your past experiences of sex industry work. Your identity is multifaceted, and you have the power to shape which parts of your narrative are highlighted as you move forward. For creating a meaningful rewarding life which reflects your true values and goals, focus on your own personal growth, self-care, building healthy support networks, and intentional changes.

In conclusion, your transition from the sex industry to the mainstream world will be a transformative journey. Your specific challenges and opportunities for growth will depend mostly on the choices you make along the way. By embracing change and prioritizing self-compassion, you can successfully navigate this transition and build a fulfilling life outside of the sex industry. Trust in your abilities, stay focused on your goals, and remember that you are worthy of happiness and success.

CHAPTER 2
Childhood Catalyst

As someone who was never a fan of Sigmund Freud, it bothered me greatly when I finally learned that many of my issues in life really did originate with my mother. Not in the classic "lay on the couch and tell me about your mother" way, but instead in the very real truth of how childhood brains react to subpar parenting and circumstances and then adapt faulty thinking coping patterns to feel loved and cared for among the chaos. Children's brains are resilient and create coping techniques to propagate survival. Hopefully, since I am starting by explaining attachment styles, you will understand more about how your early life influenced your adult life, and that might increase your self-compassion moving forward.

People come from various backgrounds and have varied reasons for choosing this line of work. It is important to reiterate that there is no single, predetermined childhood experience which leads to entering the sex industry. However, there are some common factors and childhood experiences that have been strongly correlated with sex industry workers independent of whether the work was by personal passionate choice or part of a forced nightmare. These are correlated (which means there is a high overlap between these factors and then later going into sex work), but they are not deterministic (which means that not everyone who experiences them will go into sex work).

- Economic hardship: If you grew up in a low-income family or one that was financially unstable, this could have contributed to you later working in the sex industry to escape poverty, pay off debt, or provide a better life for siblings, parents, or children.

- Childhood trauma or abuse: Childhood traumas and emotional, physical, or sexual abuse, impact boundaries, decision-making, and self-worth, and ultimately increase the likelihood of entering the sex industry. If you experienced childhood abandonment or neglect, that could lead to you seeking attention, validation, or control through sex work.
- Early exposure to sex work: Your early perceptions could have been influenced into sex work seeming an easy or viable option if you had family members or friends doing it.
- Lack of opportunities or support: Growing up with insufficient education or without a strong support system could result in you having limited other job opportunities.
- Substance abuse: If you had addiction or were unable to pass a hiring drug test, the adult industry has no such employment barriers. In addition, sex work usually brings in enough money to fund addiction and support a using lifestyle.
- Early sexualization: Having been exposed to sexual situations or pornography at an early age could have altered your perception of sex and relationships, which may have led to viewing sex work as an acceptable career choice.
- Dysfunctional family dynamics: If you grew up in a family with unhealthy relationships or communication patterns, that could have impacted your attachment style, self-esteem, understanding of boundaries, and may have influenced your choice to enter the sex industry.

You are now leaving sex work. However, if you recognize any of the above list as having applied in your early life, it is important that you address those things within therapy. And, if you are one of those people who has always felt a little broken, the answer to why is probably within that list, too. Your early life experiences are the most likely original catalyst with everything since added on top. You can change your occupation, but you will also need to ditch your feelings of self-blame, guilt, and shame to really change your life.

You were not responsible for what happened when you were a child. How traumas are processed by a child's brain is different than how traumas are processed by a previously unscathed adult. Adverse childhood events make you vulnerable. Attachment styles are patterns of behavior that develop during early childhood in response to the quality of the bond between you and your primary caregiver. Childhood abuse or neglect can determine your attachment style, and then that attachment style will continue to significantly influence your emotional well-being and relationships throughout your life.

Attachment styles

A secure attachment style comes from growing up in a healthy and nurturing environment. If you grew up in such an environment you would feel comfortable trusting others, seeking comfort from them during times of distress, and being emotionally available to support them in return.

In contrast, experiencing abuse or neglect during your childhood disrupts the formation of a secure attachment and leads to insecure attachment styles. Below are the different insecure attachment styles so you can name which may apply to you:

1. <u>Anxious-preoccupied attachment</u>: If your caregiver was inconsistently available or not responsive to your needs, you may have developed an anxious-preoccupied attachment style. This style constantly seeks reassurance, approval, and attention from others, and fears abandonment. You may also experience intense emotions and have difficulty regulating them, which could make you clingy or overly dependent in relationships.
2. <u>Dismissive-avoidant attachment</u>: If your caregiver was emotionally distant, rejecting, or unresponsive, you may have developed a dismissive-avoidant attachment style. This style has a strong need for self-reliance and independence to the extent of avoiding emotional closeness with others. You may have

difficulty confiding your feelings or trusting people, which can create distance within your relationships.
3. <u>Fearful-avoidant attachment</u>: If you were neglected or abused by your caregiver, you might have developed a fearful-avoidant attachment style. This style is characterized by both a fear of rejection and desire for emotional closeness. You may find it difficult to manage your emotions, struggle to trust people, experience frequent intense anxiety and mood swings, and have a pattern of pushing people away even when you crave connection and support.

When I first learned about this, I thought, "I knew it; I am broken!" Maybe you recognized yourself above and thought the same. But it does not have to be that way. We cannot fix something unless we can label it, and maybe now you have. Understanding your attachment style and how it has contributed to negativity in your life is a great step because your attachment style is not set in stone. With a therapist, you can work to heal and develop a more secure attachment pattern. This will require working through your childhood neglect or traumas and then reprogramming a new way to relate to others. Yes, it is possible to increase your emotional security and build healthier relationships with the help of a therapist who specializes in attachment theory and trauma. You *can* break many of your unhealthy life patterns.

CHAPTER 3
Stigma

This chapter will dive into how the effects of stigma you faced while working in the sex industry continues even after quitting. Stereotypes are generalizations about a *population as a whole* and are often—but not always—negative. So, what exactly is stigma? Stigma is the negative beliefs and judgement response to *things or actions*. Here we will focus on the stigma that surrounds those who have engaged in sex industry work.

As a sex worker, it is important to understand the difference between the stereotypes associated with your profession and the stigma you may experience because of that association. These two concepts are related but distinct. For a more detailed explanation, I will give an example that shows the difference between stereotype and stigma as it relates to strippers:

<u>Stereotypes about strippers</u>: The common stereotypes about strippers include assumptions about your appearance, personality, intelligence, and motivations.
- Appearance: Highly attractive, physically fit, and always dressed provocatively.
- Personality: Overly flirtatious, promiscuous, and attention-seeking.
- Intelligence: Lack education or intellectual abilities.
- Motivations: Solely motivated by money, trapped in your profession due to financial struggles, or drug addicted.

<u>Stigma experienced by strippers</u>: The negative attitudes, discrimination, or prejudice that you might encounter due to societal disapproval and judgment of strippers.
- Moral judgment: Stripping is typically judged as

immoral or unethical, leading to negative perceptions of those who work in the industry. People assume you lack morals and ethics.
- Discrimination: People unfairly judge you without even knowing you based on your occupation and treat you with disrespect.
- Stereotyping: The stereotypes mentioned earlier can reinforce the stigma you experience as a stripper. People make assumptions about your character, intelligence, and motivations, leading to further discrimination and prejudice.
- Social isolation: Due to the stigma, you may face social isolation. Friends, family, or potential romantic partners might respond with further judgment and distance themselves from you because of your profession.

This is an example of stigma (negative judgment) associated with the stereotypical stripper. Chances are this is not new to you. You know you have experienced judgment from others. The stereotypes and stigma for prostitution are worse. While there is much overlap between the stereotypes and stigmas faced by those who worked as strippers versus those who have engaged in prostitution, there are also distinct differences. Here I will compare the stripper versus prostitute stereotypes and stigma:

Stereotypes:
- Nature of work: The primary difference is based on the actual work being performed. Prostitutes trade direct sexual services for payment, whereas strippers perform erotic dances and entertain customers without sexual intercourse. This distinction leads to more intense stereotypes for prostitutes, who are often perceived as more immoral than strippers.
- Legal status: In many regions, prostitution is illegal, while stripping is legal. Due to this legal difference, prostitutes are often considered criminals or lawbreakers.
- Safety: Stereotypes about prostitutes frequently

emphasize that they experience violence, abuse, or exploitation from clients, pimps, or third parties. Strippers, on the other hand, are generally not associated with the same degree of physical danger.

Stigma:
- Severity: Due to the direct sexual nature of their work and the illegal status of prostitution in many places, prostitutes tend to face more intense and pervasive stigma compared to strippers. This stigma results in more severe discrimination, judgment, and social isolation for prostitutes.
- Criminalization: In places where prostitution is illegal, the stigma of engaging in criminal activity further contributes to a negative perception of prostitutes. Therefore, being viewed as a lawbreaker who contributes to societal problems worsens the stigma.
- Health concerns: Prostitutes are stigmatized due to health worries that they will transmit sexually transmitted infections (STIs) due to the extra risk from their work. This stigma creates a perception of being "unclean" or "unhealthy," which is less often associated with strippers.

In summary, the key differences in stereotypes and stigma for prostitutes compared to strippers largely stem from the type of work, the legality, and the danger and risks with their work. These factors contribute to the more intense stereotypes and stigmas faced by prostitutes compared to strippers.

Stigma makes life more complicated for stereotyped populations to start anew. Whether you fit the stripper category, prostitute category, or one of the other categories that fall under the adult industry umbrella, you have decided that you now want to live a different life. Not personalizing the stereotype and stigma associated with your past is key for your self-esteem going forward and for feeling successful in life. Now we will take a closer look at some of the ways stigma can continue affecting you even after leaving the sex industry.

The effects of stigma on individuals leaving the sex industry

Social isolation. It is human nature to want to be around others and feel like we belong, yet one of the most immediate and profound effects of stigma when leaving the sex industry is social isolation. This is due to both real and perceived stigmas associated with the sex industry, plus outward and inward judgement. Stigma and a lack of understanding complicates building connection and strong relationships with others. Transitioning is tough enough before adding on the experiences of being disconnected from your community, ostracized, and alienated due to societal attitudes and judgments. It can make building supportive networks and engaging in social activities extra challenging for former sex industry workers for many years afterward. This can be lonely.

Difficulty accessing services. The stigma surrounding sex work and the fear of being judged or discriminated against because of it can prevent you from seeking help or disclosing your past experiences. Having inadequate health, housing, or adequate alternate employment are barriers that can prevent a successful transition to a new life.

Internalized stigma. You know that old saying, "Sticks and stones may break my bones, but words will never hurt me"? As it turns out, that is not entirely true. If you are exposed to stigmatizing attitudes over and over again, you will eventually adapt and internalize those negative beliefs about yourself. They manifest into feelings of shame, guilt, and self-blame, which are counter-productive for anyone trying to build a new life. Unshakable stigma is detrimental to your self-esteem and mental health.

Mental health struggles. As if leaving the sex industry was not already challenging enough, the stigma surrounding it can lead to mental health struggles. It is not uncommon for people trying to quit to feel so judged by the outside world that they return to sex work. The non-stop judgments and obvious discrimination by mainstream society against you can exasperate pre-existing stress, anxiety, and depression. Worsened mental health is a huge roadblock that can prevent forging the required stability for change and building a new fulfilling life. For this reason, sex workers commonly self-medicate with alcohol or drugs in order to accept themselves, be artificially happy, self-soothe, and cope with so much judgment.

Hindered career opportunities. The stigma associated with sex work can complicate your ability to secure employment in other industries. Trying to find a job can be tough for anyone, but it is much harder when you have a background in the sex industry. The difference in income potential between sex work and traditional jobs is often significant since many sex workers do not have advanced education or vocational skills to qualify for the higher-paying mainstream jobs. And, if you do, the stigma attached to sex work could make employers hesitant to hire you—even when you have the skills and qualifications needed for the job. This is due to their concerns over potential reactions of customers or coworkers when they discover your past. Employers worry that your reputation may hurt the company's reputation. Just like the catch-22 of needing experience to get a job but not being about to get experience without a job, you cannot build a reputable present because people prefer to associate you with an irreputable past. Talk about unfair, right?

Impact on relationships. Stigma can also take its toll on personal relationships, both while in the adult industry and also long after you quit. Friends, family, and romantic partners may not understand or struggle to accept you which can strain your relationships or end them altogether. Due to fear of losing important connections, you might feel compelled to hide your history. It might be a constant worry that important people in your life will negatively judge or reject you.

Reinforcing stereotypes. The common stereotype of strippers, prostitutes, and porn actors is that they are inherently immoral or somehow damaged. People likely assume that you did drugs, lied, cheated, and stole, too. It is as if one negative moral choice makes you guilty of all others. The more people who verbalize the stigma surrounding sex work, the more stereotypes continue being harmfully reinforced and perpetuated. It has become socially acceptable to reinforce the stereotype that sex workers are ruined. Marginalizing and devaluing former sex workers does more than simply state your occupation is an unacceptable choice; it sends a clear message that you are a "less than" deviant who cannot possibly live up to normal societal standards and will always be unworthy of common respect. This kind of blatant underlying degradation, discrimination, and judgment of the sex industry as a whole makes it difficult for individuals who have quit to assert their worth and dignity. You are a person no matter what you do or did for work and all people deserve respect.

Legal consequences. The law is not exactly on your side after leaving the sex industry. In some jurisdictions, the stigma surrounding sex work is reinforced by punitive legal systems that criminalize various aspects of the industry. Prostitution often leads to a permanent criminal record, which results in additional barriers for accessing essential services and opportunities. However, the legal consequences from a history of working in the sex industry is not only for those breaking the law. Even within legal occupations where no laws were broken, such as working in strip clubs, massage parlors, and performing in porn movies, many jurisdictions require licensing to create permanent record documentation of your involvement in the sex industry. These licenses are a searchable paper trail which may later be used against you in custody battles, employment background checks, and even by defense attorneys if you are a victim in a rape or assault case. Legal systems that document and criminalize aspects of sex work serve to reinforce the stigma, creating even more barriers to a successful transition.

Reluctance to seek help. Stigma attached to the sex industry could make you hesitant to seek professional help for trauma, substance abuse, or mental health concerns even after quitting. This would result in inadequate care, which is never helpful for anyone trying to move forward. Your fear of being judged or misunderstood by doctors, therapists, and even police and judges is valid because stereotypes and stigma really do exist. Have you heard "All strippers are crazy." or "You can't rape a prostitute."? Of course, you have and so has everyone else. Many people believe those statements, and it is exactly this stigma that makes people in the industry afraid to seek help. To top it off, often when sex workers do seek help, frequently they are not taken seriously enough to receive assistance nor considered credible enough witnesses to warrant justice.

Perpetuating cycle. The closed doors you will face while attempting to leave the sex industry and access support, build relationships, and secure employment can make it more difficult to establish a stable, fulfilling life. These challenges can increase the likelihood of you returning to the industry or engaging in other risky behaviors as a means of coping with the stigma and its consequences. This vicious cycle is a direct consequence of stigma.

The importance of addressing and overcoming stigma

Thus far, we have delved into the numerous ways stigma affects those exiting the sex industry. It is now time to discuss the significance of confronting and surmounting this stigma. Tackling stigma is more challenging than it sounds; countless books would not be dedicated to the subject if it were possible to summarize in a mere page. Learning to manage stigma can undoubtedly improve your emotional well-being. However, there are numerous other compelling reasons to confront and triumph over stigma, such as fostering a more fulfilling and joyful life for yourself!

Through challenging your negative beliefs and seeing yourself in a more positive light, you will gain confidence, boost your self-esteem, and empower other aspects of your life. Your old life is now your old life. Even if you have been buying into the stereotypes yourself (which is common), I want you to consciously choose to shift those judgmental thoughts out of your mind and move on. No matter why nor how long you worked in the sex industry, it does not have to define who you are now. Stop judging who you were and redefine who you are now to yourself; others will eventually see the new you.

Stigma can profoundly affect your personal relationships, too. By acknowledging the stigma and addressing it candidly with your loved ones, you will be able to discern who genuinely supports you; take steps to strengthen those bonds. Some conversations may be nonjudgmental and validating from the outset. Others might require an explanation of your journey into that lifestyle, who you were before, during, and whether that differs from who you are now (make sure you spent time on the step above first). A small percentage may choose that they no longer want you in their lives because they cannot handle it, or because they are more concerned over how others will judge them for accepting you. While unavoidably painful, let them go. It is their loss. As a strong, confident, honest person who is willing to discuss who you are now, it is their loss if they choose to abandon the relationship. You deserve better than that—no matter how many times you have heard otherwise. Build a solid support network of people who accept you for you.

By confronting and reducing stigma, you are empowered to unlock new opportunities and create a brighter future for yourself. Yes, it can be terrifying to have your past on display. I get that. During the time I was in the sex industry, I mostly owned up to my role. Since I was surrounded by people who knew and I lived in Las Vegas, I did not notice the stigma while I was in that industry. That said, once I left both the adult industry and Sin City and tried to live a normal life, I realized that I was judged for my past. It was harsh. I would like to say that I was strong enough to confront that head on, but that is not what happened. Instead, I moved away, I made all new friends, and told nobody.

Then, something I had never considered as a possibility

happened. Someone from my past outed me. I was forced to admit to who I had been, both to myself and slowly to others. Let me tell you, the first few people I told, I was literally shaking with the expectation that they would judge me, and our relationship would forever be changed. And that did happen, but not how I expected. Yes, I instantly lost a few people who judged me without even caring enough to hear my side. But...the love and acceptance which came from others after I explained my past was truly shocking to me. It was the opposite of what I had always been told would happen by the people throughout my life who controlled me through shame. This was when I learned that people who deserve to be in your life will validate your current strengths and lift you.

Since stigma can create all sorts of barriers when it comes to finding work, accessing services, and getting involved in the community, you may need to create these opportunities from scratch. What skills did you learn while working in the adult industry? Can't think of any? Marketing, advertising, communication, accounting, negotiation, the ability to create rapport, patience, the ability to deal with difficult people, resiliency, instinct, fashion, beauty, etc. In order to create success in a new career, identify your strongest traits and then match them to fields you have personal interest that utilize those same traits. For example, many adult workers go on to later get degrees in counseling or nursing because they enjoyed talking to and helping people. Others go into marketing or commissioned sales because they enjoyed and were good at the negotiation aspect. By embracing the specific skills you learned along the way, you can use them in a new way now.

Often people do not even try to empathize with adult industry workers due to a lack of personal experience with those workers and a reliance on stereotypes. By discussing your occupation, you can teach others what it was and what it was not. One of the best ways to tackle stigma is by promoting understanding. When people learn more about the realities of the sex industry and the challenges faced by those still participating, leaving it, and having already quit, they are more likely to be supportive and less likely to judge you. That's a win for everyone!

During my prime, I was on a flight and the gentleman next to me asked me what I did for work. Instead of simply telling, I pulled out a business card showcasing a photo of me wearing a thong bikini and handed it to him. Clearly, I should have asked him what he did first. He was an extremely high-ranking official within a well-known church. At this time, I was still an atheist (I now identify as Christian), so I asked him numerous questions regarding his religion and quizzed him on what I perceived to be contradictions. He was very polite to answer and explained his perspective to me. I learned a lot on that flight. He also asked me many questions about my occupation, and I answered him. He admitted that I was the only person in my profession that he had ever met; and, given his status, I believe that was true. He told me that he was going to share our chance meeting and details of our conversation with the elders of his church. We both learned so much that day and each of us shattered some pre-existing stereotype beliefs.

Who cares the most within any given industry to advocate for change when it comes to the laws governing their right to work, safety conditions, pay, and how others view them? Obviously, those who work within that industry. Whether you had a positive or a negative experience, you most certainly have opinions on how things are now versus how things should be changed. If you have a passion that pushes you toward policy reform or raising awareness about the challenges faced by those who remain in the industry, your voice counts. You are in a unique position to be able to use your personal experience and knowledge to fight for a more just and compassionate society.

Creating a sense of belonging in the "normal" world can be difficult after sex work. You may have natural instincts or impulses that are not considered normal. You may feel like you cannot share because people are so different than you. Those wanting to quit sex work are faced with the conundrum of being accepted by others within the industry and being judged by most everyone outside of it, even after quitting. Unlike alcoholism or other stigmatized conditions, support groups for former sex workers to interact with others who have also quit to live happier lives barely exist. In all reality, most former sex workers who live happy lives do so by walking away from that lifestyle completely. Because, as with alcoholism, keeping your established group of friends instead of creating an all-new support system can be bad for self-esteem and cause relapse. In addition, for those who walked away and told nobody, have sex industry friends could tarnish their current reputation.

You have read about how stigma contributes to a vicious cycle of challenges and setbacks for those leaving the sex industry. Even if you cannot alter the external, you do have the power to change how you personally feel about being stigmatized. The natural reaction is depression, anxiety, or stress. But when you learn to love yourself and accept yourself, your mental health will flourish, and the external stigma will turn into jumpable hurdles. Yes, it might be harder to get a job or to gain trust, but sex workers are not the only ones who have that problem. By working on your internal self, you can come to peace with who you are and gain the inner strength to forge forward despite the hurdles, ultimately leading to a healthier and happier life.

CHAPTER 4
Guilt, Shame, & Self-blame

As previously discussed, stigma plays a leading role in the challenges you will face after leaving the sex industry. To better understand where this stigma comes from, you need to take a closer look at society's wide spectrum of opinions and attitudes on sex work. One of the most common debates around sex work is whether it is morally acceptable. Some people view it as a legitimate profession, while others see it as immoral or harmful. Diversity within beliefs usually stems from individual personal values, religious indoctrination, or cultural background. And the opinions people claim to hold may even vary depending on who their audience is at that moment. The multiple views and inconsistencies make navigating life after the sex industry a bit of a rollercoaster. Difficult as it may be, you should not permit other people's judgments to define your own self-worth.

Society often paints those involved in the sex industry as either victims or empowered individuals. Let's face it, the media plays a huge part in shaping society's attitudes towards sex work. From movies to news stories, portrayals of the sex industry are often sensationalized to perpetuate stereotypes which reinforces the stigma surrounding sex work. People believe sex workers are either destitute streetwalkers, drugged strippers, trafficked minors or kidnapped foreigners who have been victimized by pimps...or they are empowered independent high-end call girls, pampered sugar babies, and famous porn stars. These portrayals reflect the reality of some people's experiences in the industry, but not others. There is no one-size-fits-all narrative. Maybe one or more of those fit your experience, maybe none do; either way, these are the stereotypes people generally will assume about you unless you tell them otherwise.

In much of the world, prostitution and other sex work is legal or decriminalized. In most of those countries, sex work is a considered legitimate work as opposed to pimping which illegal and viewed as human trafficking. Human trafficking is akin to slavery and, therefore, is generally judged negatively almost everywhere. The differing legal perspectives can significantly affect societal attitudes and shape the public's opinion about the industry's legitimacy and the people who work in it. It is also noteworthy to mention that sex workers and their clients are held to a double standard. Whereas sex workers are often judged as immoral, their clients usually elude responsibility. The sex industry is like any other business: demand feeds supply. Sometimes those who scream the loudest in opposition to sex work are actually the clients. To top it off, the age-old inequality of men being viewed in a positive light for their sexual prowess and number of sexual partners versus women being viewed negatively for the same adds to the stigma faced by many sex workers and creates added shame for those leaving the industry.

To create a more understanding, the conversation around sex work must change. This can happen through promoting open dialogue, sharing your experience, and educating others about the realities of the industry. It is through education and advocating for change that stigmas are challenged, and a more inclusive and empathetic society is created. When we question harmful attitudes and stereotypes, we pave the way for positive change. Often people prefer to keep their past secret, yet advocacy by those who feel strong and healthy enough after their own healing is greatly needed.

Internalized stigma

When we absorb society's negative attitudes towards us or our pasts, accept those beliefs, and then internalize those beliefs toward ourselves, that is called internalized stigma. Internalizing stigma leads to self-doubt, emotional distress, and low self-esteem. Overcoming it requires an acknowledgment of our altered thoughts and feelings and identifying that we are indeed stigmatizing ourselves.

One of the first steps to recognizing internalized stigma is to become aware of the language you use when speaking about yourself or others who are in similar situations. Pay attention to whether you are using derogatory terms or adopting a negative societal view. Do you ever make generalizations about yourself based on stereotypes? Being mindful of the words you use as you frame your experiences will help you in uncovering your own internalized stigmas.

When you feel a sense of shame or guilt about your past experiences or associations, you are internalizing stigma. These feelings can manifest themselves as a persistent belief that you are somehow undeserving of love, success, happiness, or are flawed in some way. Remember that your past does not have to define who you are now. You must stop judging yourself based on who you were instead of who you are now.

Are you a hermit or socially introverted? Were you always that way or was there a catalyst? Experiencing social isolation or avoiding social interactions can be mere introversion, a reaction to trauma, or it can be a symptom of internalized stigma. If you are withdrawing from others due to fear of rejection or judgment, you probably have internalized negative societal attitudes. Meditate on whether you avoid situations due to a real personal preference or if it could be due to fears caused from stigmatizing beliefs.

Self-reflection exercises, such as journaling, can help you to explore your thoughts and feelings more deeply, which in turn will allow you to uncover negative beliefs that could be affecting your well-being. For those who have difficulty with self-reflection, hiring a therapist, a coach, or taking part in support groups might be the solution. Discussing and verbalizing your experiences with others can supply valuable insight and guidance.

After you have found which stigmatizing beliefs you have about yourself, write them down. By keeping a written log, you are taking an active step to prevent later forgetting or pretending that this is not a problem. Then, write a pro/con list to help you actively challenge these beliefs. On one side, write down any evidence that supports your negative beliefs, and on the other side write down whatever contradicts them. Take time to do this because one side will naturally be easier to fill out than the other. This requires patience and may require you to frequently go back and add new entries over a couple of days to get an accurate reflection. Are your beliefs based on facts or societal stereotypes? Evaluating the accuracy of your beliefs is a valuable tool for helping you determine whether they are rooted in reality or influenced by internalized stigma.

Self-compassion is another effective strategy for challenging stigmatizing beliefs. Remind yourself that everyone has unique experiences and circumstances, and it is crucial to approach yourself with kindness and understanding. Treat yourself the same as you would treat a close friend; your own internal dialogue should be forgiving, supportive, and loving. Give yourself credit for your accomplishments and allow yourself to feel pride in your strengths and achievements.

Evaluate your support network. Are the people you surround yourself with supportive and understanding individuals who help you to counteract the effects of internalized stigma? If not, why not? The friends you choose, the family members you spend time with, and any support groups you attend should validate you as a person, encourage you, and help you better understand your feelings. Worded another way: it is important that your closest connections help you to foster self-acceptance and reinforce positive beliefs about yourself.

Education and knowledge are empowering. By learning more about others' experiences within broader societal contexts, you develop a more nuanced understanding of your own situation. This knowledge can help to dispel misconceptions and reinforce that you are not alone. When you catch yourself internally stigmatizing yourself, listen to other people who have had similar experiences—yet are further in their healing journey. This can be particularly useful for helping you to recognize toxic thinking and then energize you forward with proper healing steps.

Finally, advocacy goes both ways. It is extremely helpful to find an advocate who can walk with you during your healing journey. The earlier you do this, the better. Having this type of support is especially helpful for anyone who was trafficked because, in the beginning, an advocate may be one of the few people who understands without judgment. There are many organizations which offer free mentorship or advocacy for survivors of human trafficking. While plenty of sex workers chose this work for their own reasons, a substantial portion have been trafficked either by pimps or relationship partners. If you suspect you may have been trafficked, then you probably were. Seek an advocate and talk about it. The other side of advocacy is the opportunity to help others after you are healed. By sharing your story and fighting against harmful stereotypes, you would be able to help others in similar situations while simultaneously reinforcing what you have learned within yourself. Challenging societal attitudes and advocating for change, whether individual-by-individual or on a grander scale, can be a powerful way to crush your own internalized stigma.

In conclusion, identifying any stigmatizing beliefs you hold about yourself is a crucial step towards healing and self-acceptance. Be mindful of your thoughts, feelings, choice of words, identify and challenge your negative beliefs, practice self-compassion, and seek external support.

Overcoming self-blame, guilt, & challenging negative self-talk

The emotional responses of guilt, self-blame, and negative self-talk hinder personal growth. The goal with challenging negative self-talk and overcoming negative feelings is to reframe your thinking patterns through a combination of self-awareness, self-compassion, and proactive strategies. The first step is notice with curiosity any emotions that arise. At this stage, you are simply an observer responsible for paying attention to what your instinctual thoughts and emotions are. Acknowledge that feelings are a natural part of the human experience, and everyone has them. By identifying and labeling your emotions, you end up creating a safe space for self-exploration and understanding.

Developing this self-awareness is essential for finding the root causes of self-blame and guilt. When you understand the triggers and underlying beliefs that contribute to these negative feelings, you can begin to challenge and reframe your thought patterns. Reflecting on your past experiences and recognizing how emotions originate will help you to understand why you have been prone to self-blame and guilt.

Once you have found the root causes of your self-blame and guilt, cultivate self-compassion. Self-compassion is treating yourself with the same kindness, understanding, and empathy that you would offer to a loved one. Practicing self-compassion is the opposite of negative self-talk and develops a more balanced perspective toward your experiences and emotions.

Challenging your negative self-talk means paying attention to and disputing your irrational and unhelpful thoughts. This process can be facilitated by asking yourself questions that promote rational thinking like, "What strong evidence supports this thought?" or "What would I say to a friend who was experiencing this situation?" When you examine your thoughts through an objective lens, you can stop the cycle of negative self-talk.

Regularly remind yourself that your worth is not diminished by shortcomings or mistakes. There is a lot more to you. A strategy for overcoming self-blame and guilt is to focus on your strengths and accomplishments. Acknowledging and celebrating your successes reinforces a positive self-image and counteracts feelings of unworthiness or failure. Self-forgiveness is a powerful tool for overcoming self-blame and guilt. Forgiving yourself for past mistakes and perceived failures can help you let go of lingering negative emotions. Forgiveness as a process for moving forward with greater self-compassion and understanding takes time.

Sharing your feelings and experiences with others can provide you with valuable insight, alternative perspectives, and encouragement. It is beneficial to actively seek support from friends, family members, or mental health professionals. Surround yourself with individuals who are supportive of who you want to be and are understanding of your emotional journey. Monitor your current negative self-talk and consistently engage in activities that actively promote self-care and well-being to stave off feelings of self-blame and guilt. Self-care activities that improve your overall mental health and resilience are exercise, spending time in nature, practicing mindfulness, meditation, nurturing personal interests, and engaging in hobbies that bring you joy and satisfaction.

To recap, overcoming self-blame, guilt, and negative self-talk is a process that requires self-awareness, self-compassion, and proactive strategies for fully reframing your thinking patterns. You can develop a healthier and more balanced relationship with yourself by acknowledging and observing your emotions, identifying the root causes of your self-blame and guilt, cultivating self-compassion, challenging negative self-talk, focusing on your strengths and accomplishments, practicing forgiveness, seeking support, and engaging in self-care activities.

Focusing on strengths and accomplishments

What do you most enjoy doing? What are your top skills? Which qualities do people compliment you on? When you focus on your strengths, you boost your confidence and improve your self-image. Make a written list of your abilities to reinforce your positive self-image. Whenever you achieve something (big or small), take a moment to recognize and celebrate your success. Figure out how to use your top strengths at work, in your daily life, during pastimes, and within your social life. For an even greater sense of accomplishment, set goals related to your strengths and further develop those skills. The more you use your strengths, the more confident and capable you will become.

By showcasing your strengths and sharing them with others, you can form connections while positively affecting their lives as well. To enhance your personal growth, seek role models who excel in your areas of strength, as they can teach you and provide valuable insight. Pay attention to their feedback on your abilities and take their feedback to heart. Embrace challenge and go outside of your comfort zone because each obstacle you overcome is more proof that you are capable. Document your achievements in writing and revisit them whenever necessary to bolster your self-esteem.

Finally, always be kind to yourself. Keep in mind that nobody is perfect! Even when you are focusing on your strengths, there will be times when things do not go as planned. In such moments, treat yourself with care and remember that setbacks are an inherent aspect of life. Focus on the good moments, surround yourself with positivity, and be kind to yourself. The company you keep and the places you frequent do matter, so choose wisely. Allocate time for activities that enable you to unwind, feel good about yourself, and recharge.

Healthy boundaries

Boundaries might pose a challenge for you due to the nature of the profession. Sex work often necessitates pushing, blurring, or compromising personal boundaries to accommodate clients' needs. Additionally, the social stigma associated with sex work can lead to feeling isolated, rejected, or judged and may impact your confidence to assert your own boundaries. Furthermore, past experiences involving trauma, abuse, or coercion while working in the industry could hinder your ability to recognize, communicate, and enforce personal boundaries in your post-industry life. It is crucial to acknowledge these factors when working towards establishing and maintaining healthy boundaries in your personal and professional relationships.

Feelings of shame, guilt, or low self-worth can complicate

asserting personal boundaries, especially if you are accustomed to feeling undeserving of respect or care. I won't sugarcoat it, there are definite power dynamics struggles that occurs within the sex industry with clients, managers, and sometimes even other people within the industry who have control or influence over your decisions. As a result, reprogramming to believe that you are now autonomous and able to make the decisions for yourself while forcing others to respect them can be tough. This is even more true when an old, familiar pressure exists. You might have had to compromise your own boundaries for financial reasons to secure a client or achieve a financial quota. Within the sex industry, there are less boundaries and people regularly do things that would not be acceptable in everyday normal life, so having your boundaries pushed might be normal for you. This makes it difficult to understand where your hard line should be. If we ask friends who are in the industry, they often do not have good boundaries either. And finally, you might have been traumatized —either before entering sex work or during, often both — and trauma can cloud your ability to establish and maintain healthy boundaries.

Now that I have covered the reasons why you might need extra help with boundaries, I want to discuss what boundaries are, how to establish them, and how to enforce them. In simple words, boundaries are basically the "rules" or limits you set for yourself within your everyday life and within your relationships with other people. Boundaries keep you feeling safe, respected, and in-control of your own life. Maintaining healthy boundaries is important for your physical, emotional, and mental well-being.

You must decide what your own values, needs, and limits are. Think back on your past experiences. All of them. Work-related, family, personal relationships, and friendships. By identifying the times where you felt extremely uncomfortable, you will know that that is a place where there should have been a boundary or there was one that was crossed. Some boundary violations are obvious, like being assaulted, being stolen from, or being cheated on. When your boundaries are weak, other people may be shocked by the boundary-breaker's behavior. When other people think someone should not be in your life, they are probably seeing obvious unacceptable behavior that you have been brainwashed to accept. Use these experiences to help you understand what you need to do for yourself and what you need from others to feel respected and secure.

Now, to establish those boundaries, it is all about expressing yourself. Communicate with the people around you to let them know what you need and where you draw the line. Make sure you are clear and assertive without being aggressive. For example, you could say something like, "Hey, I would love to be friends, but please do not call after 9pm because that is my time, okay?" And always remember to respect other people's boundaries too – respect goes both ways! Sex industry work naturally pushes boundaries, so it is possible that you may also be guilty of not respecting other people's boundaries. Pay attention to that and monitor yourself.

Sticking to your boundaries can be overwhelming or tricky at times. You will be pressured by others, and you might feel guilty about setting limits. This is when you must remind yourself that your needs matter. Be consistent with your boundaries. If you are wishy-washy about your boundaries, some people lose respect for you and intentionally violate your boundaries, while others may be confused by the ambiguity and accidentally do so. Compared to big boundary violations, smaller ones may seem acceptable to you...but they are still not. Boundaries sometimes change over time as you grow or reassess your values, but they should never change because of someone violating them. People need to respect your boundaries at all times—and that includes you, too.

Every now and then, there will be someone who refuses to stop pushing your boundaries. This is a red flag and a sure sign that you need to take a step back and reconsider whether that relationship is actually good for you. That relationship probably needs to be severed. Crossed boundaries feel bad and, the more someone crosses a boundary and gets away with it, the more they will do so in the future. In the rare cases where you do not have the choice of kicking someone out of your life completely, you can still limit your time together and emotionally disconnect from that person. Surrounding yourself with people who respect and support you will help you build a powerful sense of self-worth. When you understand your worth, it is easier to stand up for yourself and ensure your needs are met.

Engage in activities you enjoy, take care of yourself, and surround yourself with positivity. Maintaining healthy boundaries is a journey that takes time and practice. When you realize you let a boundary slip, fix it immediately and tell the person that boundary will not be tolerated to be crossed again. And then follow-through and do not permit the boundary crossing. This is what practice looks like and it gets easier and easier each time. By staying self-aware and persistent, you will create an amazing foundation for strong, respectful relationships.

CHAPTER 5
Support Systems

Building a support system:
Establishing connections for a healthy transition

It is so important to have a safe support system and establish new connections when transitioning away from sex work. Having people around you who understand and care for you can make all the difference in the world. So, let's start with the basics: What is a support system? A support system is a group of people or available resources that provide you with emotional support, practical help, or financial aid. Strong support systems can help you manage difficult situations, cope with stress, and achieve your goals. It takes intention to build a healthy support system, mutual effort, and the ability to differentiate between healthy and toxic relationships.

I cannot stress enough just how essential it is for you to recognize the value of a strong network of friends, family, and organizations. If you grew up in an unhealthy or unloving environment, it might be tough to understand why relying on others can be a strength. Humans are meant for attachment and together you can do more and be happier than succeeding on your own. There are a lot of good people in the world, but you have to push away the toxicity to befriend them. And you will see that by surrounding yourself with people who believe in you, your transition will be much smoother. Having a good social support network can make the difference in whether or not you stick it out to win your own proverbial race.

First, only focus on cultivating close relationships with individuals with whom you can trust and rely on. Choose people who share your values, are supportive of your goals, and are willing to supply constructive criticism when needed.

To increase the odds of finding such people, you can join likeminded organizations, hobby groups, sign up for interesting classes/workshops, or volunteer within your community.

Include therapy in your new support network. A good therapist can help you learn to set proper boundaries and will point out faulty thinking. There may be things that you do not want to confide with friends yet need to work out. Your therapist is someone you know you can trust and say anything to who will never later turn on you; take advantage of the unique discussions you can have. Be open and honest about your needs and what you are comfortable discussing. Your therapist is there to help you heal. This honesty will help foster stronger, more meaningful therapeutic relationships.

The healthy way to develop new friendships is slow and steady. Invest short periods of time in public places before trusting to meet in private. Slowly get to know each other. Put effort into building new relationships by meeting up for 30-minute coffee, attending events together, or engaging in activities that you both enjoy. Build trust over a long time and watch for consistency. After each brief meeting, evaluate whether that person still belongs in your life. If the butterflies in your stomach are taking over, you might not be assessing the situation correctly. The signs you need to be looking for are whether that person shows a consistent streak of reliability, respect, caring about your needs and relationship balance. Once you mutually agree that you are close friends, regular communication will foster healthy long-term connection.

If you are interested in taking up a new hobby or learning a new skill, join classes or clubs in your area to meet new people who share your interests. Local classes are a fun way to spend your time as you transition into your new life. Volunteering is another terrific way to establish new connections. Engaging in community projects or helping local worthy organizations can put you in touch with like-minded people. As a bonus, volunteering can also give you a sense of accomplishment, improve your self-esteem, and will look good on your resume.

Next, consider searching out support groups or workshops specifically designed for people transitioning out of the sex industry. These spaces provide an opportunity to meet others with similar experiences who relate to the challenges you are currently or will soon be facing. You can learn from each other's stories, offer encouragement, and build lasting friendships. There are often many toxic people in support groups, and with time you will start to see it. Seeing it in others comes before you see it in yourself. And finally, do not forget about the power of online communities! There are numerous forums, chat rooms, and social media groups where you can connect with people. Instead of gravitating to what you already know, try something new that you want to incorporate into your life. Of course, take precautions to protect your privacy when interacting online. And remember that support groups are not a suitable place to make friends, but they are ideal for working on yourself and receiving support in a safe space without judgement.

Since a lot of people have weak boundaries, I will explain something else. You know when you meet someone new, at once hit it off amazingly well and are instant best friends or lovers? Well, that is not healthy and actually demonstrates poor boundaries. Yep. I have done that throughout my life, and it felt amazing in that moment. The problem is that it lets in more false friends than true. And often those relationships will end in drama. Remember, our focus with a support group is not to collect friends or find a booty call, but to find people who will stick with us, help us, and be positive influences in our lives. This is one of those things that you might need to reprogram within yourself.

Toxic relationships hinder your progress and damage your mental health. To differentiate between healthy and toxic relationships, pay attention to how you feel when you are around certain people. Do you feel supported and uplifted, or drained and exhausted? Do your interactions leave you feeling positive or negative about yourself and your goals? Toxic friends may be obviously unsupportive, judgmental, or critical, and can undermine your confidence and progress. Others can covertly accomplish the same. Sometimes we really like toxic people, they can be fun, or we become addicted to the toxicity aspect, but toxic is toxic. You must reject toxicity to heal.

Both healthy and toxic relationships affect your mental and emotional well-being. Toxic relationships cause you to feel stress, anxiety, and become negative. It someone causes you to feel stressed out or unhappy 20% or more of the time, consider that relationship toxic. And finally, your behavior will usually worsen around toxic friends. If you find that you are gossiping more, drinking or using drugs, or doing anything while around friends that you generally disapprove of, those are toxic friends. As you leave the adult industry, you may notice toxic people will be attracted to you like a magnet and they can seem like the most accepting and easy people to get along with. Put up a STOP sign. These people are attracted to drama and a lack of boundaries. Cutting off toxic friends is not a loss; it is a choice to move forward with healthy boundaries.

How to find new non-toxic friends if they are not what you naturally attract? Begin by reconnecting with any non-toxic friends or family members you previously lost touch with. Reach out and let them know you are going through a transition and could use their understanding and support. You might be surprised how willing they are to be there for you. Then, slowly go through the suggestions at the beginning of this chapter. Do not rush friendships.

Be aware that you might be toxic, so check your own behavior too. We can usually recognize the toxicity in others when we really look, but rarely do we turn that magnifying glass back on ourselves—and you must. It is tough but necessary. Should you realize that you are toxic, that does not mean you should surround yourself with toxic friends. Discuss in detail how to heal your own toxicity with your therapist.

In conclusion, it is important to be cognizant of how toxic relationships undermine your progress and only prioritize relationships that leave you feeling positive and empowered.

Building a healthy support system is an essential part of achieving personal growth and navigating life's challenges. Healthy relationships leave you feeling heard, understood, and validated. By focusing on cultivating close relationships with trustworthy individuals who share your values and goals, you will create a supportive network that can help you achieve your dreams.

CHAPTER 6
Intimate Relationships

This section will be about romantic relationships going forward. If you are already in a healthy relationship, this does not apply to you.

New partner who already knows about your sex worker past

Before discussing relationships themselves, let's start with how a potential partner might view you if they know you did sex work.

There are common thoughts and concerns potential partners have when they know you used to be a sex worker. Of course, reactions can vary greatly as they depend on personal values, beliefs, and experiences. Being that you are interested in dating, be aware of what might be going through your new potential love interest's mind:

First, it could all be fake. A high percentage of people view having sex for free with a sex worker as a conquest, a trophy, or a sign of greatness on their part. This is crappy, yet true. The good thing is few people will invest much time to do this. By having a set amount of time that you will wait before having sex with a new partner, you can generally weed out those players. In the beginning, I decided on a no-sex/no-oral/no-nudity rule for the first 3 months, although over time it has gotten much longer. One thing I have learned is that you should never tell a potential partner how long your timeline is because then they will just wait out that extra known time, and it still will not be an emotional connection on that person's end. It will be just sex and you will get used. Since you are reading about a relationship here, you probably do not want to be used as a free prostitute. Someone who really likes you for you will patiently wait however long it takes without pressuring you or knowing the timeline.

Second, a potential partner may worry about your sexual health or any potential exposure you could have had to sexually transmitted infections (STIs). In today's world where more than 20% of people have an infection at any given moment, this is a fair concern. Many STIs do not have symptoms so testing is the only way to be sure. Few people get tested as frequently as sex workers, which means a majority of the population assumes they are infection-free without proof. It is also possible that you might be clean, and the worried new partner might not be —I have had that happen. The best way to solve this awkward concern for your partner while respecting your own health is to insist that you both go together for complete sexually transmitted infection testing before becoming intimate. When you each have results in hand, those results speak for themselves.

Your partner could be concerned about any emotional challenges you would have faced during your work and how that might affect your relationship. Sex workers have a stereotype of coming with a ton of baggage that caused them to enter that line of work to begin with. Being honest about your feelings can help a lot here. If you have baggage, being open about it is the only way to find out if the person will be able to handle it. And if you do not have emotional baggage, acknowledging your partner's potential concern about that will go a long way.

This is a weird catch-22. Partners want honesty, yet when you are totally honest and share things that many other people would have kept secret, it makes some partners wonder, "If she told me that, I wonder what she is hiding." They likely assume you only revealed the very tip of an iceberg. It makes no logical sense that honesty can foster a lack of trust from the other person, but that does happen, and I have experienced this myself. If you really are being honest with your partner, it won't take long to be clear, and trust will quickly develop. When it does not, it might be a red flag that your partner is actually the one who is guilty of not being honest and that is why trust has been too difficult to establish. Pay attention to this because a partner blaming you for not trusting you is a form of gaslighting.

Now, there is no denying that sex work comes with a ton of a social stigma. Partners may be concerned over how their friends and family will react after finding out that they are dating you. New partners could also have a legitimate worry about whether having a relationship with you could result in negative repercussions for them since judgment by others could actually affect their professional lives, custody arrangements with their own children, or even result in them being socially outcast. Depending on where you live, these could all be valid concerns.

Potential partners are often either turned on by your past experience or intimidated by it. They might wonder how your past will affect your expectations of them, role expectations, and how the dynamics within the relationship could be different. They may have difficulty accepting what you did without having serious jealousy issues. There may also be concerns over whether you (or they) are capable of emotionally bonding or if it would just be fake. And a biggie is the sexual compatibility concern; potential partners may have serious worries over you being disappointed or possibly even grading their performance in bed.

Money matters to most people. A potential partner may have two financial stability concerns when considering a potential relationship with you. First, many sex workers were financially unstable or have a lot of debt. People may not want to date you if they feel like your debt will become theirs. And second, the stereotype of sex workers is that they will do almost anything for money, so potential partners may be suspicious of whether you are using a dating relationship to financially take advantage. Not to say either of these are the case, yet it is good to know what might be running through that person's mind.

A potential partner may have concerns about whether your

past work is truly in the past or if there could be a possibility of you returning to sex work in the future. The rude phrase "You can't turn a whore into a housewife" is so common that many people believe it. Again, this either goes back to the partner's insecurity or the two of you do not know each other well yet. You should make time to have a discussion about your past work, why you stopped, whether or not it is possible you would ever return, and if so under what circumstances.

Just remember that honest conversations are the key to addressing any concerns your partner has. Dating a former sex worker can be intimidating; be aware and sensitive to that. At the end of the day, finding a partner who can love, accept, and support you for who you are is the goal.

A new partner who did not know about your sex worker past

At least half of sex workers leave the adult industry and never admit to anyone that it was ever a part of their lives. Whether you disclose your past to a potential partner is a personal decision that is usually based on several factors, including your own comfort level, the nature of the relationship, and your partner's values and beliefs.

If you do not tell, everything might go fine. Maybe the person will never find out. But…that is unlikely. Before you decide not to tell, at least think about how your partner could react if he finds out from someone other than you that you used to do sex work. Of course, the nature of your relationship and your partner's personality, beliefs, and values will factor in. These are the most likely scenarios:

1. Your partner may feel hurt, betrayed, or lied to if they learn about your past from someone else. They will know that you intentionally kept this information from them and may question the trust and honesty in your relationship.
2. The partner may confront you to confirm what they discovered and ask for clarification about your past.

This is an opportunity for honest communication, allowing you to share your experiences and address concerns.
3. Your partner may understand that disclosing your past as a sex worker is a difficult personal decision and could potentially empathize with the reasons you chose not to share this information earlier.
4. Some partners might be angry because of their own negative beliefs regarding sex work and their new judgement of you. This reaction would likely lead to extreme tension within your relationship or a breakup.
5. Needing time to process the information and reassess feelings about you or your relationship is another possible scenario. This could be temporary or be the end of your relationship.

Before you choose not to tell, think about how you will respond in each of these scenarios. This is a sticky situation; you may now be emotionally invested yet lose your relationship over it. If you find yourself in this situation, please have an open and honest conversation, empathetically acknowledge your partner's feelings, and address all concerns raised. From a partner's perspective, he may not even be sure who you are or what kind of risk you may have created.

How to tell a new partner about your past

If you are not the type to want to backpedal after-the-fact or you value starting your relationship with full honesty, then telling up-front is the only way to go. This is not easy. Discussing having a past occupation as a sex worker with a new partner requires thoughtfulness, self-awareness, sensitivity, and bravery.

Before starting the conversation, spend time reflecting on your personal journey and growth since leaving the sex industry. Consider how your experiences have shaped you and contributed to the person you are today. This self-awareness will help you to communicate more effectively and confidently with your partner.

It is likely that your partner will have preconceived notions or misunderstandings about the sex industry. Be prepared to discuss and address these misconceptions while supplying context for your experiences. Your partner may want to understand the reasons you entered this type of work, the circumstances surrounding your decision to leave, and know about any support or resources that aided in your transition. Emphasize the positive aspects of your life since leaving the sex industry. By going into detail about professional accomplishments and personal growth, your partner will have an easier time understanding that your past experiences are just one closed chapter in your life story, and you have grown and changed since then.

If your partner becomes emotional or upset during the conversation, offer empathy and reassurance. Validate their feelings and express your understanding of their concerns. You might say, "I understand that this information might be difficult for you to hear. Since I care for you, I feel it is important to disclose this early because honesty and trust are essential for healthy relationships." Take note of your partner's body language and emotional cues during the conversation to judge comfort level and gauge when it might be appropriate to pause or change the subject.

Find a balance between honesty and discretion. You can share general information like the type of work you did and for how long without going into explicit detail. You might even explain how your past has influenced your approach to communication, trust, or intimacy. Knowing these things can provide valuable context for your partner to be able to better understand your needs and boundaries.

Emphasize the valuable lessons from your past experiences and how they have contributed to your personal development. By illustrating your resilience and adaptability, you can help your partner see that your history has shaped—but does not define—your present self. Additionally, encourage your partner to openly share and discuss his or her thoughts and emotions concerning the information you just shared. Promoting honest communication will help nurture a deeper sense of trust and understanding within your relationship.

Be prepared for the possibility that your partner may need additional time or space to process the information. Provide the necessary space, extend understanding and support, and make it clear that the conversation can resume after some time has passed. If your partner is having difficulty accepting your past but is willing to work on it, couples' counseling can be helpful in addressing challenges as they emerge. On the other hand, if your partner is unable to cope with it or does not want to, it is best to unearth this sooner rather than later. Yes, it may be painful, but you deserve better than to be with someone who will not accept you for you or who would feel ashamed to claim you as a partner.

Finally, remember that disclosing your past experiences as a sex worker is an act of courage and vulnerability. By sharing this information with your partner, you are demonstrating your commitment to building a strong, honest, and supportive relationship. Trust in your resilience and strength…and remember that your past does not define your worth and you can move on to a great future.

How to disclose your permanent STI to a new partner

This is a super awkward one. If you have a permanent sexually transmitted infection, you really must self-disclose your condition before putting any new potential romantic partner at risk. Few people ask if others are clean; they just assume that others will voluntarily do the ethical thing by telling them if they are not infection-free. While that may seem stupid to not protect themselves better, it is reality that most people naturally will believe that others are good—and you should not take advantage of that. While it is true that some people really do not care about their health, most would appreciate a heads-up in advance and the opportunity to decide if the risk is worth it. Navigating this kind of conversation requires courage, empathy, and understanding. Below are suggestions to help you approach this discussion with care and sensitivity:

First, consider the timing of your disclosure. While it is important to be honest with your partner early in the relationship, you might want to wait until you two have already established a foundation of trust and emotional connection before discussing your positive status. Supportive environments foster easier and honest communication. However, waiting until after you have been physically intimate is unforgivable. You must show respect for this person by disclosing in advance of risk exposure. Condoms lower risk but do not eliminate risk completely and any potential partner deserves zero risk with you unless they have agreed otherwise by pre-informed consent. Things can go quickly in the heat of a moment, so plan to have this conversation as early as possible to avoid a much more awkward conversation later.

Ground yourself and connect with your emotions as a precursor to the disclosure conversation. You like and respect this person, and it is not fair for you to take away someone else's choice of whether or not to accept the risk. Remind yourself of the importance of transparency and respect when building strong, healthy new relationships. It is normal to have anxiety and fear of rejection. And it is possible that this person will no longer want to be with you after your disclosure. That said, your infection status is your infection status, so you need to find a partner who is willing to accept you as you are.

Whether you are disclosing herpes, hepatitis C, or HIV will make a big difference for how the conversation goes. As you share your condition, be mindful of the language you use to describe your infection. Avoid using stigmatizing or negative terms, and instead, focus on providing factual information about your condition. This can help create a more open and nonjudgmental atmosphere for discussion. Share what life has been like for you having this infection, including any challenges you have faced, support you have received, and coping strategies you have developed along the way. This will humanize your experience while also supplying valuable context for your partner.

By emphasizing your concern toward maintaining your partner's well-being, your partner will probably be willing to listen. Discuss the advice or recommendations you received from healthcare professionals when you were diagnosed and explain how you follow those guidelines. Your partner may have their own misconceptions or fears about sexually transmitted infections and you should acknowledge them. Encourage your partner to ask questions, express their thoughts, and validate their feelings as they arise. Your disclosure was unexpected and not a positive surprise, so have patience and understanding. You knew this was coming, but your partner was caught off guard and has not rehearsed how to respond.

Admit fears, shame, or guilt that you feel due to having this infection and how that could potentially emotionally impact your relationship. For example, if you get herpes on your lips you can say, "When I tell you I cannot kiss you due to a cold sore coming on, please respect that. You do not need to increase your distance, and doing so will just make me feel like a rejected leper. I am telling you now out of respect, so I hope you know that I will continue to respect you and will not intentionally jeopardize your health." By sharing in that way, your partner's safety concerns will lessen because you are clearly prioritizing safety for you both. If you have an infection where medication can lower the risk of infecting others, share whether you are taking that medication. If there is a medication that can lower your partner's risk, provide that information.

Be prepared for a range of reactions from your partner. They may be accepting and supportive, or they may need time and space to process what they were just told. Regardless of the response, it is important to approach the situation with empathy and a willingness to work through any challenges together. Reassure your partner that you value the importance of maintaining open communication throughout your relationship, whether it is about infections or any other difficult topic. Encourage dialogue and check-ins to ensure both you and your partner feel supported and informed about any changes or updates.

If your partner has difficulty processing the information, struggles to accept your infection, or if you end up infecting your partner, consider seeking couples therapy or counseling. A trained professional can help facilitate open communication and provide guidance and support for both you and your partner as you navigate any challenges that arise. Be gentle with yourself and your partner as you navigate the complex emotions that may arise during these conversations. It is ethical and brave to share your infection status with someone new. The same resilience, respect, and trust you utilized to self-disclose are the same relationship traits that will help you build a loving, supportive relationship.

CHAPTER 7
Toxic Others

You've been outed

For those of you who always kept your private life private or who started over where nobody knew your past, it can be extra traumatic if someone outs you. You had a web of emotional safety, and someone pulled the rug out from underneath you. This could be to only one person, or it could be to everyone. Facing the difficult reality of being outed for your past involvement in sex work can be incredibly challenging and emotionally taxing. To help you navigate the complexities of this situation, consider the following suggestions to help you cope and regain control of your narrative.

First and foremost, your past experiences do not define your worth or your future. You will likely feel sadness, anger, and possibly even lingering feelings of shame or guilt. You are more than your past, and your personal growth and resilience are valuable aspects of your character. Take whatever time you need to process these emotions. By addressing and confronting your feelings, you can work toward self-acceptance and healing. Grant yourself permission to grieve this loss of privacy and control over your personal story.

Remember that you have the right to privacy and dignity. As you begin to process the initial shock and hurt that comes with being outed, remind yourself that it took courage and strength to start over. You still have those qualities within you. While you cannot control what other people do, you can choose how to respond and reclaim your own narrative. Decide which aspects of your past you are comfortable discussing and with whom. By setting clear boundaries, you can protect your emotional well-being and maintain control over your narrative. Your past does not define who you are today.

If you decide to publicly address the situation, be mindful of the message you want to convey and the verbiage you use. Be authentic and honest, while maintaining a sense of self-respect and dignity. You might choose to share your story or simply acknowledge your past experiences without going into detail, depending on your personal boundaries and comfort level. You should only share details about your past if you feel comfortable doing so. Think about whether it will help people understand and have empathy, or whether it will make them further judge you.

Seek solace with friends and family who appreciate and respect you for who you are, while continuing to cultivate relationships that uplift and empower you. Please also consider reaching out to support groups or online communities specifically for individuals who have been involved in sex work. These spaces can provide a safe environment for you to connect with others who have faced similar challenges and offer guidance, understanding, and empathy. When you do not have anyone to speak with, journal your thoughts. Also, if you do not already have a trauma therapist or a therapist who specializes in sex workers, this would be a good time to find one to help you with crisis management for when you are overwhelmed or retriggered as a result of being outed and to develop a self-care plan. By creating such a plan, you will be more prepared and in control of your emotional responses.

If you have not already looked into online former sex worker support, you can check these resources to see if any are appropriate for you:
- Pineapple Support - **https://pineapplesupport.org/**
- The Cupcake Girls - **https://www.thecupcakegirls.org/**
- St. James Infirmary - **https://stjamesinfirmary.org/**
- PACE Society - **https://www.pace-society.org/**

If what the person did was purposely malicious in nature

(or if you have not yet been outed but have received threats regarding that person outing you), consider reporting the incidents to the appropriate authorities. It is worth speaking with an attorney to protect your rights and well-being and to see if that person's actions could be considered harassment, extortion, cyberstalking, or bullying. If you are experiencing harassment, threats, or other forms of harm as a result of being outed, you need to make quick decisions for your own safety and mental health. While I am not an attorney and cannot give legal advice, I will share the four types of common threats which I have observed or personally received:

1. Assuming your job is not fully legal, someone may threaten to turn you in and have you arrested. In most jurisdictions, you cannot be arrested for prostitution if you were not caught red-handed by the police. However, if you are still doing illegal sex work and are reading this book because of threats, this threat is a real concern, and you may not have any recourse other than to quit before getting yourself in legal trouble.
2. You have children and someone is threatening to turn you in so you will lose custody. This one is tricky. If your job is legal, you are providing a good safe environment for your children, and you do not have a substance abuse problem, it is highly unlikely that you would lose custody. However, if any of the three things I just mentioned are not the case, you could potentially lose custody. Judges want children in emotionally and physically safe environments, so a parent earning income by breaking the law, not providing a good environment, or having drug or alcohol problems are all reasons that your children can be taken.
3. You may have legal protection if the person is malicious and just wants to hurt you by telling others when they are aware that that you have taken steps to avoid people knowing. Many jurisdictions have laws against the disclosure of private information. Disclosing your past involvement in the sex

industry could be seen as an invasion of your privacy, especially considering that you have taken intentional steps to keep that information private. In addition, since revealing your past as a sex worker would cause you emotional distress or harm your relationships, reputation, and career prospects, you might be able to file a civil lawsuit for intentional infliction of emotional distress due to that person's extreme and outrageous malicious actions.

4. Someone who assumes that you do not pay taxes may threaten to turn you in to the tax authority. In the United States, you are expected to pay taxes on all income, whether legally or illegally generated. IRS Publication 17 states, "Income from illegal activities, such as money from dealing illegal drugs, must be included in your income on Schedule 1 (Form 1040), line 8z, or on Schedule C (Form 1040) or Schedule C-EZ (Form 1040) if from your self-employment activity." Yes, it may hurt to give up such a portion to the government. But realize that the government is not another pimp. Paying taxes is a cost of doing business for everyone.

Not paying your taxes or "cheating" on your tax filings are federal crimes resulting in prison time. Learn this important lesson from Al Capone: always claim any income you earn and pay the required taxes. If you are still in the adult business, start paying right away. If you have already quit and can afford to file amended returns and claim your income, you should do so. If you do not, the IRS can always go back three years and find any fraud. If they find any fraud within the past three years, they can then go back up to seven years. If you used your unreported income to qualify for housing, credit cards, or any loans, your application documents and payment history can be used against you. Assume that 1 out of every 3 dollars will need to be paid in taxes. Save any receipts for expenses that were necessary for you to do your job (beauty-related, condoms, hotel rooms or stage fees, track your mileage). The more valid deductions you have, the less you will owe. Keep all your receipts. If you already pay taxes and someone threatens to turn you in to the tax authority, do not stress out about it too much. Any report against you could potentially get you audited, but the IRS is much less likely to audit you if you are already claiming income.

You should seriously consider distancing yourself from whomever was responsible for the outing, anyone who threatens you, and also anyone who has made it clear that they are unsupportive of—and now judge you for—your past experiences. Focus on nurturing connections with people who demonstrate respect, understanding, and empathy. It is essential that you also define and firmly re-establish personal boundaries after such a great violation. If you are confronted by others or questioned about your past, calmly respond with confidence. Everyone has a history that shapes who they are today, and a big part of your history was your decision to quit that life and start completely over without those same choices.

When you feel ready, rebuild your personal narrative by focusing on your accomplishments, growth, and the positive aspects of your life since leaving the sex industry. Draw attention to the ways in which your new experiences have shaped you and contributed to your personal development. Engage in activities, hobbies, or pursuits that align with your values and interests, and actively create experiences and memories which are compatible with the person you are today. Maintain a focus on your personal goals and aspirations as you work through the aftermath of being outed. This will give you a sense of purpose and direction amid the temporary chaos and is a reminder of the progress you have made. Later, you might even consider using what you learn from this experience to help others through online support groups, mentorship, or advocacy as they face similar challenges.

Most people have done things they would rather others not know about, and sometimes it happens that the world finds out despite their desire for it not to. I had to totally rebuild. It is unfortunate that this outing was not on your own terms, however, it does not have to be the end of the world. I know this is painful. You have the strength and the determination to overcome this, doing so will build resilience, and you will learn who your real friends are. Try to stay focused on all your personal growth, the challenges you have overcome, the positive changes you have made, your current achievements, and continue forward toward future goals. You may need to make adjustments, but you can take ownership of your past and still be happy. Give it time and you will see...

Stalking issues

As a former sex worker myself, I am all too familiar with the unique challenges that come with the territory. Among the many risks of sex work, stalking is a particularly insidious and pervasive threat. In this section, I will delve into a range of factors that contribute to your increased vulnerabilities with being stalked and other forms of harassment. By understanding the societal and systemic issues that heighten our risk, you can work towards keeping yourself safer.

One of the primary reasons that you are more susceptible to stalking is the pervasive stigma and discrimination sex workers face daily. This stigmatization often leads to a dehumanization of sex workers, causing some people to view you as an easy target for harassment, stalking, and other forms of abuse. Marginalization might decrease your likeliness of reporting incidents of stalking or seeking help from law enforcement due to a fear of not being taken seriously, being blamed for the harassment, or facing further discrimination. Stalkers also know that others have negative views of sex workers and expect that nobody will really care nor consider you worthy of helping.

The nature of sex work involves close and intimate interactions with clients and fans. While the majority of clients are respectful and maintain professional boundaries, you also have an increased exposure to people with unhealthy attachments or obsessions, and that can lead to stalking. High-level public visibility creates susceptibility for attracting unwanted attention from potential stalkers, so sex workers with online advertising or public social media are at increased risk.

The power imbalances within the industry make you more vulnerable to stalking since you are trained to be reliant on others for your safety and have learned to accept that you have less control over your interactions. Additionally, the criminalization of sex work exacerbates vulnerability due to fear of getting in trouble if you reach out for help. To top it off, law enforcement sometimes may even try to discourage you from seeking help when faced with stalking and tell you to work it out yourself (that has happened to me).

Needless to say, dealing with stalkers is a frightening and emotionally draining experience. Not only can the stalker terrify you, but feeling as if there is nobody to protect you can make it much worse. Stalking is serious and dangerous whether in-person or online. You have the right to feel safe and secure.

Years ago, law enforcement was not very helpful when it came to stalking victims. As a sex worker, it was my experience that law enforcement and the legal system did not care what happened to me. That goes against justice. No matter what you do for work, you should not have to constantly live in fear due to a dangerous person who is out to harass you, invade your privacy, or cause you harm. Luckily, over the years, many states have passed stalking and cyberstalking laws and some even include stalking under the umbrella of domestic violence. However, even with great improvements that increase legal recourse, you can still expect to be blamed by the stalker (and possibly even by the legal system) so ensure that you provide as much proof as possible. You also need to adjust your own lifestyle to create extra security for yourself because it takes a lot of evidence before anything will happen to that person.

When someone is stalking you, it is crucial that you save all stalking evidence: call logs, screenshots of messages or online interactions, proof of hacking, and alarm system notifications. Be forewarned that sometimes saving the evidence on your device or leaving it inside your home may not be good enough because stalkers are boundary disregarders who might break into your residence to steal or hack your resources to leave you without any evidence. During my most recent stalking experience, I had forwarded my digital evidence to several friends. It is good that I did that because then my telephone and computer were both hacked and all of the evidence relating to that person was deleted. This happened two or three times before that person realized that enough other people also had copies that it would not be possible to make my evidence disappear. If you do not have friends or family to forward to, you can always save on CDs or flash drives and store them in a bank safety deposit box or get a PO Box and mail it to yourself. The evidence is important if you decide to report the issue to the authorities, file charges, get a restraining order, or seek any other kind of legal assistance due to that person. Keep a detailed record of the incidents, including dates, times, and any other relevant information.

Take control of your online narrative by being cautious about the information you share on social media and other platforms. Be mindful of the images you post, the locations you tag, and the personal details you disclose. By being selective about what you share, you can minimize the opportunities for the stalker to intrude on your life. Reevaluate your online connections, removing or blocking individuals who you do not know well or who seem suspicious in order to create a more secure network of contacts and reduce the risk of your personal information being shared inadvertently.

Be cautious about sharing personal details, such as your address, phone number, or other identifying information. This is extra tricky for someone still doing sex work or needing to advertise to get clientele. If you cannot hide your information, get familiar with the block options, and learn to better screen your clients to ensure that you are not being set up by the stalker. Other than blocking people or flagging inappropriate content for removal, ignore anything posted by the stalker or other haters. The more you act like it does not bother you, the less fun it will be for the stalker.

Start changing your passwords for everything. Then adjust your privacy settings on social media platforms and other online accounts to limit your publicly accessible information. Consider setting up new email addresses, social media accounts, or phone numbers when you believe that your existing accounts have been compromised. If that still does not work, you may need to get new devices or restore them to factory reset. Inform only trusted friends and family members about the changes to reduce the chances of the stalker accessing your new accounts.

When you have mutual friends or connections with the person stalking you, it is important to inform them of the situation so they can be aware and cautious about sharing your personal information. This prevents them from unknowingly being the leak in your life. Remember to keep your own safety and well-being as the top priority. It is also essential that you confront the person stalking you in writing with a firm and clearly stated message that the behavior is considered harassment, it is not welcome, you are not interested in that person, you want to never be contacted again, and that person should immediately cease all of the stalking behaviors. There are people who do not understand subtlety. You must be ultra clear; it does not matter if it is rude. After sending that message, you should immediately block the stalker on all of your social media platforms and other online accounts. While this may not stop the stalker from trying to contact you, it can help create a barrier and provide you with a sense of control. If the person continues, it will also create a very obvious paper trail for filing stalking charges.

Educate your friends and family about online safety and privacy measures, as they can play a critical role in safeguarding your personal information. Encourage them to review their own privacy settings and be mindful of the content they share that involves you. Develop a safety plan for when you are offline as well. If the stalker's behavior escalates to offline stalking, share your concerns with close friends and family members and establish a system of check-ins or communication protocols to ensure you remain safe. By doing that, others will hopefully be on alert and look after you. Be aware that sometimes seeking support from friends or family can go either way. Gaslighting is not uncommon for stalkers and sometimes your family and friends may actually be convinced that you are the one who is crazy, occasionally even believing that the stalker is the victim! It is so sad when loved ones opt to believe that you must be crazy instead of believing that a charismatic person could be dangerous. That is a definite sign that even your circle views you as a stigmatized "black sheep." For those who are accustomed to being outcast (myself included), this feels like the ultimate betrayal by family. And the stalker will relish it!

Luckily, trauma therapists know what narcissists and sociopaths are, so therapists are much more likely to believe you. They also see how you are reacting to the situation, which will add credibility to what you are indeed experiencing. Try to limit talking about the stalker more than you need to. The more you do, the greater power you give the stalker over your mental health. When discussing your experiences with others, be cautious about sharing too many details. While it's important to seek support, sharing too much information can inadvertently provide the stalker with additional avenues to harass you or gain access to your personal life.

As you work through the emotional challenges of being stalked online, it is essential to prioritize self-care and stress management. Developing a routine that incorporates journaling, meditation, and exercise will help you to process and release the associated stress. Take breaks from your online presence. Disconnecting from social media and other online platforms as needed can create an opportunity to recharge and focus on your well-being away from the stressors of the digital world. Remember that your feelings and emotions are valid, and it is okay and normal to feel overwhelmed, angry, or scared in the face of online stalking. Acknowledge these feelings and allow yourself the space and time to process and heal. Be patient with yourself as you work through the emotional and practical aspects of coping with a stalker. Healing and regaining a sense of safety and control may take time, but you have the resilience and strength to overcome this challenge.

A stalker's actions are completely a reflection of his own dysfunctional issues and are not a result of anything you have done or who you are. You cannot force anyone to stalk you and someone doing so is not your fault. There are several national organizations in the United States that specialize in assisting victims of stalking or online harassment. These organizations offer resources, support, and guidance for victims:

- National Center for Victims of Crime (NCVC): The NCVC operates the Stalking Resource Center, which provides resources and support for stalking victims. They offer information on stalking laws, safety planning, and various resources to help victims cope with their experiences. **https://victimsofcrime.org/**
- National Domestic Violence Hotline: 1-800-799-SAFE (7233). The National Domestic Violence Hotline offers 24/7 support to victims of domestic violence, which can include stalking. Trained advocates are available to provide confidential support, resources, and referrals to local services. **https://www.thehotline.org/**
- Cyber Civil Rights Initiative (CCRI): 1-844-878-2274.

CCRI focuses on online harassment and nonconsensual pornography (also known as "revenge porn"). They offer a crisis helpline, resources for victims, and advocacy to raise awareness and promote legal reform. **https://www.cybercivilrights.org/**

- Love is Respect: 1-866-331-9474 Text: "LOVEIS" to 22522. Love is Respect provides support, resources, and advocacy for young people affected by dating violence, including stalking. They offer a 24/7 helpline, online chat, and text support. **https://www.loveisrespect.org/**
- Without My Consent: Without My Consent aims to combat online harassment, nonconsensual distribution of intimate images and online impersonation. They provide resources for victims

- and educational materials to promote awareness and understanding of the issues. **https://www.withoutmyconsent.org/**
- Working to Halt Online Abuse (WHOA): WHOA is a volunteer organization dedicated to helping victims of online harassment and cyberstalking. They provide resources, assistance, and advice for dealing with various forms of online abuse. **https://www.haltabuse.org/**

Please note that the availability of resources and support will vary depending on your location. This is just a starting point; you should research local organizations and agencies in your area that can provide assistance tailored to your circumstances. Lastly, hold onto hope and trust in your own ability to reclaim your life and well-being. While dealing with online stalking can be a deeply distressing experience, you possess the strength, determination, and resourcefulness to confront and overcome this adversity.

Types of digital real-time stalking and how to protect yourself

Digital stalking, also known as cyberstalking, is a growing concern in today's connected world. It refers to the repeated, unwanted, and intrusive monitoring, harassment, or threats directed at you through digital means such as social media, email, instant messaging, or other online platforms. It is essential to be aware of the different methods of digital stalking and the steps you can take to protect yourself from potential harm.

The most common form of digital stalking involves using social media platforms to monitor and track your activities, relationships, and personal information. The stalker may obsessively follow your profiles, comment on your posts, or send you unwanted messages. In some cases, they may even create fake profiles to interact with you or those connected to you. It is often possible for your connections to figure out your current location through the social media application's location tracking features.

Another type of digital stalking involves using email or instant messaging platforms to send you unwanted or threatening messages. The stalker may intimidate or harass you through relentless communication, often leaving you feeling vulnerable and overwhelmed. Digital stalkers may also engage in doxing, which involves gathering and publishing your personal information online without your consent. This can include your home address, phone number, workplace, or other sensitive details, potentially exposing you to additional risks and harm. In some cases, digital stalking may involve hacking into your online accounts, devices, or networks to gain unauthorized access to your personal information, communications, or other personal data. The stalker may even post pretending to be you to damage your life or simply just to let you know they got in. This type of invasion can be particularly distressing, as it leaves you feeling violated and uncertain about your safety and privacy.

If you receive unwanted or threatening messages, resist the urge to respond or engage with the sender. Instead, immediately document the messages by taking screenshots and saving copies, and also block the individual from contacting you further. Keep a detailed record of all instances of digital stalking, including dates, times, and descriptions of the incidents. This information will be helpful if you decide to report the issue to the authorities or seek legal assistance. If the stalking behavior escalates or you fear for your safety, you really should file criminal charges against the stalker. You have the right to feel safe and secure, both online and offline.

Cyberstalking is a serious issue so, if you are a victim, it is important to take steps to report and address it. Reporting cyberstalking can involve multiple channels, depending on the nature and extent of the stalking. I have personally contacted all of these at one time or another (the FBI instantly solved my problem, although it required me letting them into my life to a higher degree than I was comfortable with). Here are the general guidelines on where to report same-state and interstate cyberstalking:

- Local law enforcement: Your first step should be to report the cyberstalking to your local police department. They will make a report, provide suggestions for what you should do, and hopefully they will investigate. Make sure to provide your supportive evidence when filing the case. Get the case number and file updates if the person continues to stalk you.
- State law enforcement: For same-state cyberstalking, you can also report the incident to your state's Attorney General's office or the state police.
- Federal law enforcement: For interstate cyberstalking or cases involving severe threats or harm, you can report the incidents to federal law enforcement agencies. The Federal Bureau of Investigation (FBI) investigates cyberstalking cases, especially those that involve death threats or cross state lines. You can file a complaint with the FBI's Internet Crime Complaint Center (IC3) at **https://www.ic3.gov/**.
- Online platforms: If the cyberstalking is taking place on a specific online platform, such as social media, messaging apps, or forums, report the user and the incidents to the platform. Most platforms have reporting mechanisms for abusive behavior and can take action against the perpetrator, such as suspending or banning their account. The platform will usually also request to see your proof.

There are internet resources and support networks that provide guidance and advice for coping with online stalking. These resources include webinars, articles, forums, and support groups specifically focused toward helping individuals navigate the complexities of online harassment. If the stalker continues to harass you through different accounts or platforms, then look into advanced tools like IP address blockers and browser extensions designed to help you identify, track, and block the stalker's activity and protect your online privacy.

If the stalking behavior escalates or you fear for your safety, don't wait to contact the appropriate authorities, which could be the police or a specialized cybercrime unit. They can provide guidance and support toward helping you to address the issue and protect yourself. Remember that it is essential to keep records of all the incidents related to cyberstalking, including screenshots, messages, and any other relevant evidence. This documentation will help law enforcement agencies and online platforms to investigate and take proper action. Stay strong, take the initiative, and trust in your ability to protect yourself and reclaim your sense of safety and control in the digital world.

Wireless networks, such as Wi-Fi networks, can be used to track your real-time location. Your device constantly searches for available networks, and each network has a unique identifier that can be used to locate your device. Unless you are using a VPN, the internet network you connect to may provide a lot of information to anyone who understands networks. Another way that stalkers can track your location is through GPS-enabled devices. These include fitness trackers, smart phones, and even Air Tags since they constantly transmit location data, which can be accessed by stalkers who gain unauthorized access to your device or account. To top it off, many mobile phone apps grant permission to track your GPS location data, too, so be cautious and read the fine print for each app before installing, and only allow access when absolutely necessary.

Bluetooth can also be used to track your location data when your Bluetooth devices are connected to your smartphone or another device that has cellular or Wi-Fi capability. RFID (radio-frequency identification) technology is used in many everyday items, such as credit cards, passports, and key fobs. These devices emit a unique signal that can be used to track your location. Most people think that RFID cannot be used in that way because passive RFID cannot; but stalkers can use active RFID to track you in real time.

There are many things you can do to prevent a stalker from tracking your real-time location. Turn off location tracking on your devices and apps whenever possible. Most devices and apps allow you to disable location tracking or limit access to your location data. Check the settings on your devices and apps to see your settings and adjust them accordingly. Consider using a VPN (virtual private network) or other privacy tool to protect your online activity from prying eyes. A VPN encrypts your internet traffic, making it more difficult for a stalker to track your online activity and location.

If you have never before used a VPN, these are all well-known:
- ExpressVPN - **https://www.expressvpn.com/**
- Private Internet Access - **https://privateinternetaccess.com/**
- CyberGhost - **https://www.cyberghostvpn.com/**
- Torguard VPN - **https://torguard.net/**
- NordVPN - **https://nordvpn.com/**

Be cautious about who you allow access to your devices and accounts. Having physical access to any device is the quickest and easiest way to hack it and often will not show up on a spyware scan. Avoid sharing your passwords or allowing others to use your devices without your permission. Do not reuse the same password for multiple accounts. Enable password protection and two-factor authentication wherever possible to prevent unauthorized access and to add an additional layer of security to your accounts.

It is relatively easy to for someone to hack your phone and enable your microphone and camera, record you, or view you in real time from remote. Purchase a Mic-Lock for your phone and any other portable devices you use to prevent being eavesdropped on. Get a faraday wallet for your phone, car keys, and garage door opener. Long ago the camera covers were inconvenient, but now they are cheap and slide open and shut. Block your cameras when not in use with a camera cover. You can buy all of these items on Amazon. Disable location on your phone.

If you suspect that someone is tracking your real-time location, consider changing your routines and habits to make it more difficult for them to locate you. Vary your routes, travel at unpredictable times throughout the day, and avoid sharing your plans with others. If signs persist that someone always knows where you are, you might be being tracked through cell phone spyware, GPS device attached to your vehicle, or through active RFID.

You must remain vigilant with your safety. Be aware of your surroundings. Pay attention to whether the same vehicles appear at the various locations you visit. Notice whether there is someone in the distance watching you. It is horrible to live this way, although if you can identify the person or get a license plate that can help a lot. When you notice suspicious behavior or activity (like someone across the street from your house sitting in their parked car and using their laptop), contact the authorities. Don't hesitate to take action if you feel unsafe or threatened in any way.

Most of you reading this will not have the following experience, but unfortunately, I have so I am going to include this too. If someone has at any time had physical access to where you live without being watched, they might have had an opportunity install discreet covert cameras. They can be hidden in any room, or even in the attic looking down into your house through unnoticeable pinholes in your ceiling. It is easy to purchase devices online which can detect audio listening devices and hidden cameras and they are worth the money if you suspect that you might be being monitored in this way. The device will either provide you with peace of mind knowing that your house is actually safe, or they will confirm your suspicions and help you find evidence so you can call the police. Make sure you document the search procedure. Do not touch any surveillance equipment you find; instead, if you find evidence, call the police immediately.

As you can see, there are numerous ways that spy tools and

digital technologies can be used by stalkers to track your real-time location. It's important to be mindful of these potential risks and take steps to protect yourself from harm. By being proactive and taking steps to protect your privacy and security, you can reduce the risk of someone tracking your real-time location and minimize the potential harm they can cause. The sad reality is that sex workers are frequently stalked. You might be viewed as uncredible compared to perpetrators who often come across as respectful "good society" people. Therefore, people may not believe you, and that increases your danger.

Whenever you feel threatened or harassed, always trust your gut. Have you read "The Gift of Fear"? If not, you should definitely check it out. I did not escape sex work unscathed, but I know for a fact that what I learned from that book did save me from additional violent scenarios. The book's premise is all about the importance of trusting your instincts to stay safe. This is extra important for current and former sex workers since sex workers attract stalkers at a higher rate, so always take extra steps to protect your personal information and keep yourself safe.

Pimps

Some pimps are obviously so; but there are many more who are discreet and pretend to be the romantic partner. A lot of people in the sex industry are exploited by pimps without ever realizing that is what it was. Since understanding what has happened to us is so useful in healing, I want to explain what a pimp is and how distinct types of pimps gain control.

A pimp is a person who directly profits off of your doing sex work. This is different than a Hollywood agent who takes 15% of your booking fee. A pimp generally takes the majority or all of your money, and there is no contract to protect you from exploitation.

Some pimps attempt to deceive their victims by posing as romantic partners, but there are still certain telltale red flag signs when someone is a pimp and not your loving partner. If half of the below criteria fit, you were probably trafficked:

- Financial control: A pimp may control all aspects of your finances, including earning and spending money.
- Isolation: A pimp may isolate you from friends and family, making it difficult for you to seek help or support.
- Physical abuse: A pimp may use physical violence as a means of control over you.
- Coercion: A pimp may use coercion, threats, extortion, or blackmail to force you into doing something.
- Sex trafficking: A pimp may engage in sex trafficking, which involves the recruitment, transportation, and exploitation of you and/or others for the purpose of prostitution.
- Manipulation: A pimp may manipulate you emotionally, using guilt or other tactics to maintain control.
- Multiple workers: A pimp may have multiple workers that they use to generate income.
- Glamorization of prostitution: A pimp may glamorize prostitution, portraying it as a desirable lifestyle choice rather than an exploitative and dangerous industry.
- Exploitation: A pimp may exploit you for financial gain, using you to generate income without providing adequate compensation.
- Control over daily activities: A pimp may exert control over your daily activities, including when and where you work, sleep, and eat.
- Human trafficking: This is rarely mentioned when it comes to pimps, but many do this, too. Human trafficking is the same as sexual trafficking and pimping except the money you are earning for them was not generated through sex industry work.

There are many resources available for sex workers who want to exit prostitution and escape exploitation, including hotlines, transitional housing, and free counseling services. If you suspect that you are in a relationship with a pimp, please seek help. Remember: you deserve to be treated with respect, you are worthy of dignity, and you have the right to a safe and healthy life free from exploitation and abuse.

Each pimping style has its own characteristics and methods of operation that distinguish it from the others. Understanding these different types is helpful for those who are at risk of being exploited so they can recognize what to watch out for. If you see these signs in someone, even if that person has not tried to pimp you, keep your distance.

Gorilla (also called Guerilla) pimps are the pimp type traditionally portrayed by popular media who use force, physical violence, and intimidation to control their victims. They are often involved in other criminal activities, too, such as peddling drugs, committing robberies, extortion, and coercion. In addition, they may threaten to reveal sensitive information or harm their victims' loved ones for non-compliance of their demands. Gorilla pimps might work independently or in gangs. Gang pimps are particularly dangerous, as they have a network of other criminal associates who are willing to help them carry out their sinister operations.

Breaking free from a gorilla or gang pimp is possible with the right support and resources. Here are some steps that sex workers can take to break free (the order may vary with your situation):

- **Seek help and support from trusted individuals.** This can include family members, friends, a therapist, a support group for survivors of sexual exploitation, or a local organization that offers services to victims of sex trafficking.
- **Create a safety plan.** This should include identifying safe places to go, developing a code word or phrase to alert others to danger, and making a list of emergency contacts. Ideally, try to identify safe places to go, pack a "go bag" with important documents and necessities, and identify which people or organizations will be

able to provide support and assistance.
- **Collect evidence.** This includes text messages, emails, voicemails, or any other documentation of abusive behavior, demands for you to work, threats, or violence.
- **Contact law enforcement.** Report threats or incidents of violence to law enforcement and provide them with any evidence that you have collected.
- **Consider a restraining order.** Restraining orders provide legal recourse and make it easier for law enforcement to arrest the pimp if intimidation, abuse, posts, or contact continues.
- **Plan for financial independence.** Identify ways to earn income that do not involve sex work. Take classes or enroll in job-training programs.
- **Leave when the opportunity arises.** Take advantage of a moment when the gorilla pimp is not around and find a safe place to go.
- **Cut off all contact with the pimp.** You should change your phone number, email address, and other contact information to prevent the pimp from reaching you.
- **Stay alert and be aware of your surroundings.** It is important to remain vigilant and aware of potential danger, especially in the days and weeks following your departure.

Breaking free from a gorilla or gang pimp is a challenging, emotionally taxing, and extremely dangerous process. Law enforcement will sometimes support you in the process and offer you help and protection if you are willing to turn evidence against the pimp. Getting away without police help is riskier and more difficult. Seek help and support from trusted individuals, develop a safety plan, and take steps to protect your physical and emotional well-being as you begin the process of rebuilding your life.

Romeo pimps, on the other hand, are more subtle in their approach of using manipulation and charm to gain your loyalty and trust. They often pose as hustler friends or may even be your romantic partner. They are smooth talkers who lavish on compliments, affection, and gifts to make you feel special and appreciated. However, this affection is just a façade, as the pimp's ultimate goal is to exploit and control you for his own financial gain. Often physical force is not needed because they successfully brainwash you. Romeo pimping can be difficult to identify because, since the relationship seems consensual on the surface, you might not even realize that you are being trafficked. These pimps may make you think they are the "supportive boyfriend" who love you so much that they can handle what you are doing for work and demonstrate that by "helping" drive you to and from work, screen your clients, save your money so you won't spend it, or secure your advertising. Romeo pimps may convince you that together the two of you are saving up a nest egg so that you can eventually quit adult industry work. Then, later at the end of the relationship, you discover that they actually stole all of your retirement savings (which could be tens or hundreds of thousands of dollars).

Familial pimps are a particularly insidious category of pimps as they exploit their own relatives for financial gain. This could be your parent, sibling, or another close relative who uses emotional manipulation to control you. Familial pimps can be particularly difficult to report to authorities, as you may hold on to a sense of loyalty or obligation to your family members.

Escaping from a loved one or family member who is pimping you is emotionally traumatic. It can be tough to trust again because this person crossed a few sacred boundaries that should never be crossed. You will require long-term therapy to help you process the betrayal and traumas, reparent yourself, build new coping skills, and develop a plan for moving forward with your life. The same applies if the pimp was your partner.

When a family member or romantic partner has been pimping you, coming to acceptance is a devastating and traumatic process. You believed it was a real relationship and were emotionally invested, but instead the other person was using and profiting off of you. Your loyalty and sense of obligation has been taken for granted and met with fake connection. You may still feel connected to that person. As horrible as it is, you are not alone in this experience, and there is help and support available to you as you begin to process and cope with this realization. It can take years of intensive therapy to recover from the brainwashing you experienced.

Consider whether getting a restraining or protective order against your partner or family would be useful. If so, there are organizations that will help you fill out the paperwork and even go to court with you as your personal advocate. You should also change your phone number and other contact information to prevent further harassment or abuse. Some states even have confidentiality programs to hide your location. Legal recourse is also an option for those who want to pursue that.

In addition to your physical safety, you need to protect your mental and emotional health. Counseling can help you work through top-down trauma and feelings of shame, betrayal, anger, and any other emotions that may arise in the aftermath of this kind of trauma. Stress-reducing exercises like mindfulness, meditation, yoga, and acupuncture can help with the bottom-up processing of trauma. Art therapy and journaling are other ways to express yourself in a safe way while processing difficult emotions.

Whether you were involved with the pimp due to force or manipulation, the actions of a pimp are never the fault of the victim. You deserve to have agency over your own body and choices. By seeking help and support, practicing self-care, and prioritizing your own safety and well-being, you can begin to heal and reclaim your sense of self-worth and empowerment. Healing is a process, and it does take considerable time to fully recover from the emotional trauma caused by being pimped. There will be good days and bad days and that is normal. Take things one day at a time while seeking help and support along the way as you need it.

Escort services, massage parlors, and strip clubs are usually at-will employment. That is true unless you are being controlled or pressured by an external person or the business is a front for one of the other types of pimps. Many people who work in these locations are pimped, although it is usually by a third-party and not the business itself. Quitting work at one of these types of locations is typically easy; they anticipate you will likely voluntarily return. So many sex workers return to the business after announcing retirement that it is almost an expectation by the employer that you will, too. Therefore, the ending of these work relationships is usually cordial with an open door.

Recognizing that there are different types of pimps and knowing what they look like is a key step in protecting yourself from future exploitation and abuse. Some pimps fit into more than one category. If you suspect that you are or have been victimized by a pimp, seek help and support from a local organization that specializes in assisting victims of human trafficking and exploitation. They will be familiar with this type of situation and will not judge you. You can also confide in a trusted friend, family member, or therapist; however, they may not understand as people who haven't experienced this don't.

Let me repeat. You deserve to be treated with respect and dignity. You have the right to a safe life that is free from exploitation and abuse. Remember that assistance is available to provide support, resources, and help you escape or recover from trafficking and rebuild your life. If you or someone you know is being sexually trafficked, here are some organizations that can provide assistance:

- National Human Trafficking Hotline: 1-888-373-7888 or text "BEFREE" to 233733. Support via 24/7 hotline, chat, text and resources for victims of trafficking. **https://humantraffickinghotline.org/** and
www.polarisproject.org
- National Center for Missing and Exploited Children:

1-800-THE-LOST (1-800-843-5678). Provides assistance and resources to families and children who have been victims of trafficking. **https://www.missingkids.org/**
- The Salvation Army: Assistance and resources to victims of trafficking, including emergency shelter, counseling, and other support services. **www.salvationarmyusa.org**
- Freedom Network USA: Organizations and individuals who provide support and resources to victims of trafficking. **www.freedomnetworkusa.org**
- End Child Prostitution and Trafficking USA (ECPAT-USA): Organization that works to end the sexual exploitation of children and provides support and resources to victims. **www.ecpatusa.org**

Related to pimps, sometimes your own family can be toxic. Either they are the ones exploiting you or they will reveal information about you to the person who has exploited you. It is really crucial that you recognize this and are honest with yourself about your level of danger. In these cases, even when difficult, it is often best to cut off communication completely with your family in order to protect yourself physically, mentally, and emotionally.

For those who fell into being pimped, were manipulated, or realized after-the-fact what happened, that is an ego hit that is tough to describe. In my case, I consider myself a smart woman who did well in school, so I could not accept the reality of being so stupid. For years, I struggled to cope with the traumatic truth of what had happened. I was torn between harsh self-judgment or comfortable dissociation. Even here I just used that same word ("stupid").

Yet, thanks to much therapy, I now understand that I was not stupid—I was vulnerable. When we are vulnerable, someone who is skilled in how to take advantage of that vulnerability can manipulate us. Having a vulnerability has nothing to do with intelligence or a lack thereof. The attachment style we formed in childhood sets up our vulnerability risk.

In Chapter 2, we discussed attachment styles. Those with an anxious-preoccupied or fearful-avoidant attachment style are more vulnerable to exploitation in various forms, including being pimped. This is because these attachment styles are more susceptible to manipulation and control by others due to their ardent desire for emotional closeness and approval, coupled with a fear of abandonment or rejection.

As you probably remember, anxious-preoccupied people have a need for attention, validation, and reassurance. So, when anxious-preoccupied people are offered emotional support or a sense of belonging, they can be easily manipulated. They can overlook red flags due to a desire to maintain relationships and avoid painful feelings of abandonment. The subconscious also ignores red flags when one's childhood attachment style is getting what it needs, so they may not even be able to see exploitation warning signs that are obvious to others.

The other attachment style with an increased vulnerability for being pimped is the fearful-avoidant attachment style. These people are afraid of rejection, struggle with emotional regulation, and have difficulty trusting, yet they still have a deep desire for connection. This combination makes them susceptible to manipulation by someone skilled in knowing how to exploit those vulnerabilities. A pimp offering a solid sense of security can be so powerful that a fearful-avoidant person may cling to a toxic situation for the stable consistency despite being controlled, abused, or exploited.

I fit into the anxious-preoccupied attachment style category. This is why I was vulnerable, and that vulnerability was established during my childhood. I cautiously protected myself from obvious pimps but eventually met a caring charismatic Romeo pimp who did not fit the typical pimp stereotype; he recognized my vulnerability and knew how to exploit it. I had other toxic relationships before him, and I never understood why my relationship picker was so off until I learned about attachment styles. My parents did not intend to screw me up, but the attachment style I developed growing up with them is what created my vulnerability.

    I share my experience because many of you reading this have this same attachment style. If you were pimped, that does not make you stupid; it means you were vulnerable. And your vulnerability started at an incredibly early age. Being vulnerable was not your fault. You are not a bad person or dumb for being vulnerable. Pimps who intentionally search out vulnerable victims in order to target and exploit the vulnerable unhealed children still deep inside of them are predators. Your vulnerability was taken advantage of to make you an income source for someone else. They are the ones who are bad. Pimping is a type of human trafficking.

    I know this is probably new for you to hear because pimps brainwash and make you question everything about yourself to get themselves more power. They make you believe that you are tainted, broken, will never be accepted by others, or cannot get by without them. Forgive your past vulnerability and what you have done in your life because of it. Work on healing your attachment style now, in the present, to have a happier future.

    Our established childhood attachment styles remain our attachment styles for life unless we do the work to change them. This is why some people (myself included) have had a lifetime pattern of toxic relationships. If you identify as either of the above two styles, it is crucial that you seek help to heal your attachment style so you do not have a revolving door of exploitive manipulative people in your life.

CHAPTER 8
Career

Exploring New Paths and Possibilities

Transitioning from sex industry work into a normal job is not easy. The work environment is not only completely different, but the pay is usually significantly lower. With any luck, you had an opportunity to save up in advance for the transition. For the majority who read this, you probably did not have the foresight or opportunity to save up or maybe your savings were quickly depleted. In any case, the lowered pay of mainstream work can make normal work seem not worth it at times. It is common to want to give up. I don't say this to discourage you; I bring it up because you will likely think this yourself and I want you to be prepared to move past those thoughts in order to succeed in the mainstream world. Be aware of the negative talk and remind yourself of the advantages of leaving the adult industry.

It can be exciting to explore your interests, skills, and passions to find the perfect fit for your new future. Dedicate time to thinking about what kind of work you would enjoy doing and whether it aligns with your values and long-term goals. Reflecting on these questions in advance will help guide you toward a fulfilling new career. You should purposefully choose an environment that you can thrive in.

Education and training can be a game changer when transitioning to a new career. If you already have certifications or degrees, your job search will be easier. If not, please consider researching community colleges, trade schools, or online courses which offer programs in fields you are interested in. In the grand scheme of things, six months to two years toward training for a new career that you can support yourself with is very reasonable. Many institutions even offer financial aid or scholarships that can make education more accessible. If you have no idea what you should do, most schools have guidance counselors that will speak with you for free. You can also take a career assessment, and there are plenty of free tests online. In addition, you can find the book "What Color is Your Parachute?" at any library. It is considered the top job-hunting book and will help you identify your strengths, interests, suitable career options, write your resume, pass your interviews, and recommends appropriate courses or training programs to get you started.

Many tech companies offer free training programs that can help you gain the skills needed to work in the tech industry. For example, Google offers a range of free online training courses and certification programs in areas such as cloud computing, data analytics, and web development. Here are some examples of specific free educational opportunities that train for new vocations:

1) **Tech training programs:**
    - Professor Messer on YouTube has an entire free series that can help you learn everything needed to pass CompTIA certification exams for A+, Networking + or Security+, **https://www.youtube.com/c/professormesser**. I personally learned using his video courses and passed all of my exams. It was tough, but similar programs at tech schools cost thousands of dollars and his is free. All you need is a computer and time to learn.
    - Codecademy: Codecademy offers interactive courses in programming languages such as Python, Java, and HTML/CSS. You earn badges and certificates as you complete courses and progress through the curriculum. **https://www.codecademy.com/**
    - edX: edX is a nonprofit online learning platform

that offers courses in a variety of tech-related fields, including computer science, data analysis, and cybersecurity. Courses are offered by universities such as Harvard, MIT, and UC Berkeley. **https://www.edx.org/**
- Coursera: Coursera offers both free and paid courses and specializations in tech-related fields such as software development, cloud computing, and data science. You can earn certificates upon completion of courses and specializations. **https://www.coursera.org/**
- Udacity: Udacity offers courses and nanodegrees in fields such as artificial intelligence, cloud computing, and web development. You can earn certificates and build projects to add to your portfolio. **https://www.udacity.com/**
- Khan Academy: Khan Academy offers free courses in computer science and coding, as well as math, science, and other subjects. You can earn badges and track your progress through the curriculum. **https://www.khanacademy.org/**
- FreeCodeCamp: FreeCodeCamp offers a full curriculum in web development, including HTML/CSS, JavaScript, and Node.js. You can earn certifications as you complete the curriculum and build projects for non-profit organizations. **https://www.freecodecamp.org/**

2) **Healthcare training programs:** Healthcare is a growing industry with many job opportunities. And unbelievably, there are many free training programs available that can help you gain the skills needed to work in healthcare. For example, the American Red Cross offers free training programs for nursing assistants, phlebotomists, and other healthcare roles.
- Red Cross Certified Nurse Assistant Training: The American Red Cross offers free Nurse Assistant Training programs in several states. These programs provide comprehensive training for individuals interested in becoming CNAs, including both classroom instruction and hands-on clinical experience. **https://www.redcross.org/take-a-class/**

cna
- MedCerts Healthcare Programs: MedCerts offers free training programs for several healthcare professions, including Medical Billing and Coding, Pharmacy Technician, and Electronic Health Records Specialist. These programs provide online instruction and prepare students for certification exams. **https://medcerts.com/programs/healthcare**
- Project Horseshoe Farm: Project Horseshoe Farm is a nonprofit organization that offers free training programs for individuals interested in becoming Certified Nursing Assistants or Medical Assistants. The program is based in Alabama and provides hands-on training and support for participants. **https://www.projecthsf.org/**
- National HealthCare Corporation: The National HealthCare Corporation offers a free Nurse Aide Training Program at several locations in Tennessee, South Carolina, and Alabama. The program provides comprehensive training and prepares students for the state certification exam. **https://nhccare.com/careers/**

3) **Trade schools:** Trade schools offer vocational training programs, such as welding, plumbing, and automotive repair. Many trade schools offer financial aid or scholarships to help cover the cost of tuition. That said, there are also free trade schools:

- Job Corps: Job Corps is a federal program that provides free vocational training for eligible individuals aged 16 to 24. The program offers training in several trades, including automotive repair, construction, healthcare, and information technology. **https://www.jobcorps.gov/**
- Home Builders Institute: The Home Builders Institute is a nonprofit organization that offers free training programs in construction trades, such as carpentry, masonry, and plumbing. The program is offered at several locations across the United States. **https://hbi.org/**
- North American Building Trades Union (NABTU):

NABTU offers free training programs for individuals interested in trades such as electrical work, welding, and pipefitting. The program is offered at several locations across the United States. https://nabtu.org/
- The Iron Workers Apprenticeship Program: The Iron Workers Apprenticeship Program provides free training in structural ironworking, reinforcing ironworking, and welding. The program is offered at several locations across the United States and includes both classroom instruction and hands-on experience. https://ironworkers.org/become-an-ironworker/apprenticeship

4) **Military training programs**: The military offers many training programs that can lead to careers in fields such as aviation, mechanics, healthcare, and engineering. Many of these programs offer college credits or certifications that can be applied towards a degree. There is an age cap here: you cannot be over 42 years old.
- Army: Army Airborne School, the Army Cyber School, and the Army Engineer School. https://www.goarmy.com/careers-and-jobs/
- Navy: Navy Aircrewman Program, the Navy Nuclear Power School, and the Navy Hospital Corpsman School. https://www.navy.com/
- Air Force: Air Force Aviation Maintenance Technology Program, the Air Force Technical Training School, and the Air Force Electronics Principles Course. https://www.airforce.com/
- Marine Corps: Marine Corps Combat Engineer School, the Marine Corps Motor Transport School, and the Marine Corps Communications-Electronics School. https://www.marines.com/
- Coast Guard: Coast Guard Aviation Maintenance Technician Program, the Coast Guard Machinery Technician Program, and the Coast Guard Maritime Law Enforcement Academy. https://www.gocoastguard.com/

5) **Non-profit training programs**: Many non-profit

organizations offer free training programs in a variety of fields. For example, Dress for Success provides career development programs to help women gain the skills and confidence needed to enter or re-enter the workforce. Others are:

- Goodwill Industries International: Variety of training programs and can also help with job preparation, resumes, and interview coaching. **https://www.goodwill.org/training-and-work-opportunities-for-goodwill-programs/**
- Year Up: One-year program that provides young adults with technical and professional skills, as well as corporate internships. **https://www.yearup.org/**
- Job Corps: Free education and training program that helps young people learn a career, earn a high school diploma or GED, and find and keep a respectable job. **https://www.jobcorps.gov/**
- Code.org: Free online coding courses for students of all ages and backgrounds. **https://code.org/**
- YouthBuild: Education and training to low-income young people who want to learn construction skills and build affordable housing for their communities. **https://youthbuild.org/**
- National Youth Employment Coalition: Membership organization that works to improve outcomes for young people by providing resources, training, and networking opportunities. **https://nyec.org/**
- National Restaurant Association Educational Foundation: Training and certification programs for working in the foodservice and hospitality industries. **https://chooserestaurants.org/**
- National Center for Construction Education and Research: Training and certification programs for working in the construction industry. **https://www.nccer.org/**
- National Retail Federation Foundation: Training and certification programs for working in the retail industry. **https://nrffoundation.org/**
- National Coalition for Homeless Veterans: Job training and employment services to homeless veterans. **https://nchv.org/**

- **American Red Cross**: Training and certification programs in areas such as CPR, first aid, and lifeguarding. **https://www.redcross.org/**
- **American Welding Society**: Training and certification programs for working in the welding industry. **https://www.aws.org/education/**
- **Society for Human Resource Management**: Training and certification programs working in human resources. **https://shrm.org/LearningAndCareer/learning/Pages/EducationalPrograms.aspx**
- **National Association of Home Builders**: Training and certification programs for individuals interested in working in the home building industry. **https://www.nahb.org/education-and-events/education**
- **The National Federation of the Blind**: Training and resources for blind individuals interested in pursuing vocational and educational opportunities. **https://nfb.org/**
- **National Safety Council**: Training and certification programs in areas such as defensive driving, workplace safety, and first aid. **https://www.nsc.org/**
- **Association for Talent Development**: Training and resources for professionals in the talent development field. **https://my.td.org/search/courses**
- **National Urban League**: Training and resources for individuals interested in pursuing careers in a variety of fields. **https://nul.org/**

These lists give you an excellent starting point if you want to be trained for a new vocation and are cash-strapped. Explore and research the best fit for your individual needs and goals.

If you are looking to work right away instead of undergoing vocational training, your local unemployment office can provide you with job listings, resume assistance, interview coaching, and information about local employers. They will connect you with job opportunities that match your skills and interests. In addition, temporary agencies, like Kelly Services, are a way to get job experience early on which can sometimes lead to a permanent position.

Often people forget about the power of volunteering. There are many advantages to volunteering if you currently have the time. Not only is it an excellent way to give back to your local community, but volunteering also helps fill in your resume with job experience and lets you meet people within your chosen field who may later offer you a paid job. Be open to jobs within different industries, consider internships, or even job-shadow to get a taste for what you enjoy and where you want to focus your energy. By doing this, you might discover a passion or talent for something you would never have expected.

Networking can play a crucial role in discovering new career paths. Attending events for industries you are interested in, going to job fairs, and signing up for workshops will ensure you are able to meet more professionals in your desired field. Do not be shy about introducing yourself and asking for advice. It is also a clever idea to add everyone you meet this way to your LinkedIn page. You never know when someone might have a helpful tip or a job lead for you. Who you know is often more important than skills when looking for work.

I waited until the end to mention this, but it works best for my own personality style and might for yours. Have you ever given serious thought to starting your own business? Depending on which area of the adult industry you were in, you may already have all the business skills and know-how. So, if you have an enterprising spirit, consider turning one of your passions into an income source. Being in charge of your own small business is an empowering way to build a new career on your own terms. You can start your own mainstream business without having a boss or being subject to stigma.

Career transitions are challenging, and it can take time to find the right fit. Be patient with yourself during this process and remember that every step you take is bringing you closer to your goals. Continue exploring your options, learning, and networking. Welcome the journey of possibilities, and you will find yourself well on the way to a fulfilling and rewarding career. You've got this!

The resume

Now, let's see where you are starting. Do you have educational degrees or previous mainstream job experience? If so, that is great! Both of these will allow you to draft a resume that does not include gaps or sex work. You can also disclose your sex work if you choose to. You have the most options when there are no gaps of time.

When you have a history of sex work and are looking to transition into a "normal" job, it is important to highlight the transferable skills and experiences on your resume that you gained from your previous work. Some of the job skills that you could emphasize include:

- **Communication skills.** You likely had to communicate effectively with clients to establish boundaries and ensure their satisfaction.
- **Sales and marketing skills.** In many cases, working in the sex industry involves promoting and selling services to clients.
- **Time management skills.** Juggling multiple clients and appointments requires excellent time management skills.
- **Customer service skills.** You likely excelled at providing a high level of customer service to clients in order to build trust, loyalty, and earn repeat business.
- **Empathy and emotional intelligence.** To be successful, you had to develop emotional intelligence and empathy skills for connecting with clients and understanding their needs.
- **Critical thinking skills.** Working in the sex industry has unique challenges and obstacles, and successful adult industry workers develop outside-the-box problem-solving skills as a result.
- **Confidentiality and discretion.** Many jobs require a high level of confidentiality and discretion; these are skills that you developed due to your unique experience.
- **Adaptability and flexibility.** Adult industry work

can be unpredictable, and those who are successful develop strong adaptability and flexibility skills as a result.

By highlighting the above skills and experiences, you demonstrate to potential employers that you have valuable abilities that can be applied to a variety of job roles. Additionally, it is important to remember that many employers value diversity and actively seek candidates with a range of backgrounds and experiences. Do not be afraid to own your past experience and use it to your advantage in the job search process. Confidence goes a long way.

If you have never had a job other than sex work, you can still create a resume that will help you get a job. When you have gaps of time in your resume or have not done other work, you need to be creative. Education, volunteer work, skills, and personal interests are the other categories you can include on your resume to fill the page. Re-read that list above and then look at the sample resume on the next page. It shows how a woman without any job experience other than stripping and without an education can still create a decent resume.

Missy Moore

848 N Rainbow Blvd, Las Vegas, NV 89107
(555) 555-5555
missy@springforward.com

To obtain a challenging position in a customer service-oriented environment that utilizes my exceptional communication, interpersonal and problem-solving skills.

Experience

2014 – PRESENT
Entertainer and Customer Service / Las Vegas, NV
Experienced in providing exceptional customer service to a diverse clientele. Strong interpersonal and communication skills developed through years of experience working as a stripper at multiple clubs. Proven ability to work independently and under pressure.

- Provided exceptional customer service to a diverse clientele
- Maintained a high level of discretion and confidentiality
- Developed strong sales and marketing skills to promote and sell services to clients
- Demonstrated strong problem-solving skills to manage and resolve client issues
- Successfully managed multiple clients and appointments simultaneously
- Developed strong communication and interpersonal skills to establish boundaries and ensure client satisfaction

Skills

- Excellent communication and interpersonal skills
- Ability to manage multiple tasks and clients simultaneously
- Strong problem-solving skills
- Excellent time management and organizational skills
- Ability to work independently and under pressure
- High level of confidentiality and discretion
- Strong sales and marketing skills
- Social media expertise

Activities

- YOGA
- TRAVEL
- DANCE

CHAPTER 9
Financial transition

If you have not yet quit the adult industry, creating a budget and plan while you are still earning will make your transition significantly easier. Here is what you do:

First, figure out how much money your household will need to survive without luxuries and write down the detailed list on a sheet of paper. This means your rent, utilities, groceries, and car expenses only. No eating out, no drugs or alcohol, no shopping for items other than the most basic essentials. If you have pets, make sure you add in your realistic pet expenses, too. Pets are family. This bare-bones tally amount will be much less than you probably expected. Work until you have enough saved up for 6 months of the bare bones monthly total you previously created.

Next, to prevent spending the savings, pre-pay your rent or mortgage and car payments, purchase money orders for future utility payments, and buy gift cards for the rest (gas, groceries, etc.). Once you have done this, quit doing sex work (no part-time) and find a "normal" job that will cover your expenses. The buffer you have saved up will be "insurance" to keep you from stressing out during the transition period. Try to remain 6 months ahead and not rely on any of the buffer money...but, if you do end up needing it, that is why it is there. Within a few months, you will be adjusted to the new lifestyle, successfully budgeting your new income, and living a happy new life! If you do this as I just detailed, you will probably have a few months of unused credit left over. Try to always keep at least a 3-month safety cushion buffer to ensure you will remain financially okay even when emergencies or unforeseen circumstances occur.

Seeing how easily money comes to others makes it more difficult to live poor. Maintaining your adult industry friendships could tempt you back into the life, and this applies to both co-worker and client friendships. Also, if you do have drug addiction, alcohol abuse issues, or shopping compulsions, overcoming them needs to be a top priority so these things do not cause you to return to sex work. If you are truly serious about quitting the adult industry, you really must be prepared to give all of these things up.

The above advice was for those who still have the opportunity to make more sex industry money. I am assuming that the majority of those reading this book have probably already quit so the following many paragraphs will be about budgeting starting now.

Money comes in larger amounts and quicker to sex workers than it does for most industries. Due to the ease, lots of sex workers blow through their money and never learn how to manage or budget because there are always opportunities to make more. If you already understand savings, budgeting, investing, and have good credit, feel free to skip to the next chapter. However, if not, the next many paragraphs will walk you through the basics.

How to budget

First, in order to responsibly manage your money, you must set clear financial goals and create a written budget. To make it more interesting, attempt to estimate your expenses before creating a budget, because doing so will show you how much your estimates differ from the actual figures. It will take tracking your income and expenses for a month or two to get a clear picture of your financial situation. And I am not just talking about your basic expenses. This will be difficult, yet essential, because there are lots of additional expenses that will be left out of a quickly compiled list. You must log every dollar you are currently spending, not just the main bills. Make sure you include every impulse purchase, drive-thru meal, latte, gifts, and donations. Literally, track every dollar you spend to see where your money is really going. This is not a budget yet; you are simply observing your spending habits.

After you know how much you are actually spending each month and on what, categorize your expenses and set limits for each category while making sure to prioritize necessities like rent, utilities, and groceries first. You must stick to those limits! Pay off all expenses first. Create a written list each month and physically cross the items off as you spend the money. If you have any money left over, create a savings nest egg. Think about what you want to achieve in both the short-term and long-term, like paying off debt, saving for a down payment on a home, or investing in your education. Creating such a clear vision will help you stay motivated and focused. You might also consider creating and hanging up a vision board.

When it comes to saving and investing, the typical advice is to tell you to open a high-yield savings account, a retirement account like an IRA or 401(k), or even to explore low-cost investment options like index funds. Those options are all designed to help your money grow over time and contribute to your long-term financial stability. It is also crucial to have an emergency fund in place that can cover at least three to six months' worth of living expenses and provide a safety net in case of unexpected expenses or a sudden loss of income. Set a goal for your emergency fund and build it up over time.

Of course, I am not an accountant nor a financial adviser. And, while I know all of the words in the previous paragraph, explaining in more detail is far above my pay grade. If you do not know where to start, there is an easier way: Speak with a financial advisor! Doing so does not have to cost you money. Here are a lot of free resources for getting professional help as you learn to navigate investing:

Government websites:
- MyMoney.gov: Information on budgeting, saving, investing, and managing debt. **https://www.mymoney.gov/**
- USA.gov: Resources on managing money, taxes, and investing. **https://www.usa.gov/**

- Consumer Financial Protection Bureau: Information on consumer finance laws and regulations, as well as resources on managing finances. **https://www.consumerfinance.gov/**
- Social Security Administration: Resources on retirement planning, disability benefits, and survivor benefits. **https://www.ssa.gov/**
- Department of Housing and Urban Development: Resources on buying a home, avoiding foreclosure, and renting. **https://www.hud.gov/**

Non-profit organizations:
- National Foundation for Credit Counseling: Free credit counseling services and financial education resources. **https://www.nfcc.org/**
- Junior Achievement: Financial literacy education to students from kindergarten to high school. **https://jausa.ja.org/**
- Operation Hope: Financial coaching and resources to individuals and families. **https://operationhope.org/**
- Financial Planning Association: Free financial planning resources and connects individuals with financial planners. **https://www.financialplanningassociation.org/**
- Society for Financial Education and Professional Development: Financial literacy education and resources to individuals and organizations. **https://sfepd.org/**

Financial institutions:
- Bank of America: Free financial education workshops and webinars to its customers.
- Chase Bank: Free online resources on budgeting, saving, and credit.
- Capital One: Free financial literacy resources and a financial coaching program to its customers.
- Navy Federal Credit Union: Free financial education resources and workshops to its members.

- Ally Bank: Free financial literacy resources and tools on its website.

Online resources:
- NerdWallet: Articles, calculators, and tools to help individuals make informed financial decisions. **https://www.nerdwallet.com/**
- Investopedia: Educational articles, courses, and investing tools. **https://www.investopedia.com/**
- Khan Academy: Free financial literacy courses and resources. **https://www.khanacademy.org/college-careers-more/financial-literacy**
- The Balance: Articles and resources on personal finance topics such as budgeting, saving, and investing. **https://www.thebalancemoney.com/**
- SmartAsset: Provides calculators, articles, and resources to help individuals make informed financial decisions. **https://smartasset.com/**

Local community resources:
- Public libraries: Often offer free financial literacy classes and resources.
- Community centers: Provides financial literacy classes and workshops to residents.
- Churches and religious organizations: May offer financial counseling and resources to members (Dave Ramsey has a great online course that many churches offer to their members as a free benefit).
- Local government agencies: May offer free financial education workshops and resources to residents.
- Non-profit organizations: In addition to national organizations, there may be local non-profit organizations that offer financial literacy education and resources.

So, now you know how to get free training for gaining control over your financial life. Do not be afraid to seek professional advice when it comes to managing your finances. Not doing so can cost you money. Financial advisors or credit counselors can help you navigate your unique financial situation and provide valuable guidance on budgeting, debt repayment, and investing. Please look into utilizing these resources.

If you are self-employed, it is crucial that you set aside sufficient money for taxes, keep accurate records of your income and expenses, and file your tax returns on time. Consult with a tax professional if you are confused about your obligations and responsibilities. If you have outstanding debts, develop a strategy to pay them off as efficiently as possible which might involve consolidating loans, focusing on high-interest debt first, or using a debt snowball or avalanche method to tackle your obligations. Managing debt is a key aspect of achieving financial independence.

Credit

You are probably already aware of your approximate credit score. A good credit score can help you secure better interest rates on loans, qualify for credit cards with better rewards, and even get approved for housing rentals. Keep an eye on your credit report and take steps to improve your score by paying your bills on time and reducing credit utilization. Free credit reports do not show your actual credit score, but they will show you what has been reported.

If you know your credit is bad or if you have recently received a denial based upon your credit score, you can find out more details and then start repairing your credit. This is not exceedingly difficult, but doing so does require time, patience, and follow-through. These are the steps:

1. **Obtain and review your credit reports.** You can get a free copy of your credit report from each of the three major credit bureaus (Equifax, Experian, and TransUnion) once per year from **AnnualCreditReport.com**. Review each credit report carefully to identify any errors, check for incorrect

account information or any payments that were reported late or missed.
2. **Dispute errors on your credit reports**. If you find errors on your credit reports, you should dispute them with the credit bureaus by requesting they correct the errors while providing documentation to support your reasons. You can also contact the creditors directly to ask them to correct the errors, too. I recommend doing both.
3. **Pay your bills on time**. Pay all of your bills, credit card payments, utilities, and loans on time. Making on-time payments is the most crucial factor in determining your credit score.
4. **Reduce your credit utilization**. Credit utilization is the amount of credit you are using compared to the amount of credit available to you. Aim to keep your credit utilization below 30% of your credit limit. If you have high balances, try to pay them down as much as possible. This is the second most important factor in your credit score.
5. **Don't close old credit accounts**. Keep your oldest credit accounts open and use them occasionally to keep them active. Long-standing low-balance accounts raise your credit score. Do not close unused accounts.
6. **Limit new credit inquiries**. Applying for new credit temporarily lowers your credit score. Only apply for credit when you really need it and try to limit the number of requests.
7. **Seek help, if needed**. If you are struggling with debt, ask a financial advisor or credit counseling agency whether bankruptcy is the best choice. If it is not, create a plan to help you manage your debt and improve your credit over time.

Repairing credit takes time, patience, effort, persistence, and constantly follow-through. Even then, expect the process to take at least a few months to a few years before you will see a significant improvement in your credit score. You can take control of your credit and improve your credit score. Remain patient, be consistent with your budgeting and saving habits,

TRIXIE RACER

pay everything on time, and celebrate your progress along the way. You've got this!

CHAPTER 10
Balance

As you continue to grow in your personal self-discovery journey, you must create healthy life balance. Balance might be a new concept if you were "managed," since balance would have lowered your income potential. If you used a fake persona for work, you might have an altered idea of balance that was defined as balancing the time when you were that alter-ego versus when you were not—but that is not what I mean by balance here. You are no longer in the sex industry and need to learn a new version of balance for being a whole heathy person.

Many people function with an all-or-none mindset, and that kind of mindset can easily be adapted to allow for balance. The way to do so is to dedicate 100% of your effort when it is work time, give relationships your full attention when spending time with them, and make sure you also give yourself 100% during prescheduled self-care time. Then figure out the percentage of time for each category while still putting all of your attention toward one focus at a time. My favorite balance is 50% of my time focused on work, 35% of my time set aside for social interactions and family, and 15% dedicated to self-care. In the sex industry, many of us were trained to have a much higher work percentage. That is not healthy for long-term sustainability so learning balance is key.

Work-Life Balance

Achieving a sustainable work-life balance is an essential part of maintaining overall happiness. It can be challenging to find equilibrium, especially when transitioning to a new career or environment. Here are some strategies to help you strike the

right balance between your professional and personal life:
- Set clear boundaries: Establish distinct boundaries between your work life and personal life. This includes only being available during work hours, creating a dedicated workspace (if you work remotely) and only spending time in that space while working, and communicating your work-personal time boundaries with your employer and coworkers when needed.
- Prioritize your time: Order tasks by urgency and importance. By doing this, you will be able to balance personal and work activities. Make sure to add self-care into your schedule to ensure sufficient down time.
- Learn to say no: Doing too much will cause you to burn out. Be aware of how much you can comfortably manage, and do not take on more than that. It is important for you and others to respect your limits.
- Delegate tasks: In case you realize that you do have too much to do, ask for help or outsource some of what needs to be done to others. Proper delegation will get everything done while allowing you to focus on other activities or tasks.

Achieving work-life balance is to maintain proper equilibrium between a successful work life and a satisfying personal life. That is what it means. Neither should interfere with the other's time. A distorted work-life balance will eventually damage your mental health. Therefore, it is essential to respect yourself and your needs and make time adjustments in how you are spending your time as needed.

Relationships

Maintaining healthy relationships is a crucial aspect for social balance. Strong connections with friends, family, and romantic partners provides emotional support that enhances overall well-being. Choose to keep people in your life who are supportive and non-toxic.

Again, some of you may not need this section, although so many people in the adult industry have difficulty within their family relationships, understanding what healthy friendships look like, or both. I do not say this as judgement, I say it as a direct observation from many years within that industry. Healthy relationships contain specific nurturing aspects:

Communicate honestly. Open communication is key to building strong, trusting relationships. Share your feelings, needs, and concerns with your loved ones, and encourage them to do the same.

Develop trust. To earn trust, be honest regarding your intentions, be dependable, share your feelings, and do what you say you will do. Trust is built through consistent, reliable behavior and open communication. The people you trust should also earn your trust the same way.

Spend quality time. Make a conscious effort to schedule quality time with your friends and family. Make a conscious effort to set aside time for regular get-togethers and other shared activities that you all enjoy. The memories you create can last a lifetime.

Be present and attentive. When spending time with loved ones, give them your full attention. To engage in meaningful conversations, show genuine interest in others' thoughts and feelings, listen completely before formulating a response and do not interrupt. Refrain from checking your cell phone while with people you care about.

Set and respect boundaries. Harmonious relationships are based on mutual respect. It is necessary to set personal boundaries to protect yourself in a myriad of ways. Respecting the boundaries of others is how to show that you respect their needs and feelings. If someone else's boundaries are unclear, ask so that you do not inadvertently violate them.

Use kind words. Part of mutual respect is not insulting each other. Even when you are upset or disagree, be mindful of your words and actions. You should build up your loved ones with your words, not break them down. Joking around with disparaging words is not kind at all, even when you both laugh. Do not insult yourself either.

Address conflicts constructively. Directly address conflicts when they arise without permitting them to fester and gain added resentment. A willingness to work together openly and empathically toward finding a solution demonstrates that your relationship is important.

Be patient and forgive. Be aware that it is human nature to judge others more harshly than we do ourselves. We do not realize we do that, but we do. Therefore, be willing to forgive loved ones when they fall short and request forgiveness when you do the same. Extending the olive branch maintains healthy relationships. Strong relationships are built on a foundation of mutual effort, patience, commitment, and occasional forgiveness.

Show appreciation and gratitude. Nobody likes to feel taken for granted. Use both words and actions to ensure your loved ones know that you value their presence and express gratitude for their efforts in supporting you. Do not underestimate the value of frequent small gestures of appreciation.

Offer and accept support. Be willing to both offer and accept emotional support. Providing a listening ear, a shoulder to lean on, or practical help can strengthen your bonds with others.

Compromise. There are no relationships where people are always in sync, so make sure that compromise exists on both sides. It's not healthy when one side always wins or always gives in. Relationships require both sides periodically making concessions. Doing so demonstrates your commitment to the relationship and the willingness to sometimes put the needs of others first.

Be supportive and autonomous. Encourage your loved ones to pursue their goals and interests. By embracing them for who they are, you show support and an appreciation for their uniqueness. While it is essential to be supportive and engaged in each other's lives, it's equally important to maintain your sense of individuality, autonomy, and personal growth within your relationships by taking the time you need for yourself, too.

Prioritize self-care. To maintain healthy relationships, you must start with yourself. By taking care of your own physical, emotional, and mental well-being, you are better equipped to support and engage with your loved ones. This not only helps maintain balance in your own life, but it also sets a positive example for those around you.

Check in and be open to feedback. Periodically discuss issues, touch base, and see if boundaries need to be reevaluated. By doing this, you can usually discover problems before they blow up out of proportion. Encourage your loved ones to share their thoughts and feelings about you or your actions, listen, and then make changes as needed. Taking feedback to heart demonstrates that you value the other person's perspective and shows your commitment to the relationship. Relationships require mutual effort and caring enough about others to invest your time and energy.

Do not underestimate the power of relationships. For a satisfying personal life, you must cultivate healthy relationships. Nurturing relationships require honest and open communication, quality time together, and mutual sharing of your needs and emotions. Expressing yourself and being accepted and trusted for who you are and you accepting them in return enriches your life through strong friendship bonds. Celebrate your close relationships and all of the positives that stem from them. These joyful moments, laughter, and unique experiences create sentimental memories and make you feel emotionally supported.

Making new friends

Having at least a few friends you can count on is important for mental health. This may seem out of place, but I am including it for a reason. Just as in other professions, there are many introverts within the adult industry who either put on an act or self-medicate in order to have the courage to speak with people. After quitting, take time to get to know yourself again, which includes shedding any false personas that you created and implemented for work.

For introverts, you might naturally feel isolated and alone and unsure how to make friends. Making friends is a social skill that can improve by knowing what to do and practicing. When initiating contact with strangers, remain mindful of the situation, your body language, the way you communicate, and their reactions. Here are some tips for approaching someone new:

1. **Choose the right moment.** Observe both the person and the situation. To prevent bothering someone who is already preoccupied, engaged in a deep conversation, or showing signs of discomfort. Is this person approachable?
2. **Approach with confidence.** Walk toward someone with a confident posture and relaxed demeanor. Maintain a friendly facial expression and make eye contact.
3. **Respect personal space.** Stand at a comfortable distance, giving sufficient personal space while still being close enough to engage in conversation.
4. **Start with a friendly greeting.** Offer a warm smile and say "Hello" or "Hi" to make your presence known. This combination signals your desire to initiate a conversation.
5. **Use an icebreaker.** Choose a natural and relevant icebreaker: a compliment, a question about where you are, or a comment about something you both likely know about or have seen.
6. **Be aware of your nonverbal communication.** Maintain eye contact and ensure your body language shows that you are engaged and interested in the conversation. Do not fidget, cross your arms, or look down as you talk because that type of body language signals dishonesty, distress, and discomfort.

7. **Listening actively.** Give the other person your full attention as you listen to their response. Show that you are genuinely interested in what they have to say by nodding, maintaining eye contact, and offering verbal cues such as "uh-huh" or "I see."
8. **Build on the conversation.** Respond to what the person says by asking follow-up questions that the person would be happy to answer and which show that you are interested in getting to know them. Be genuine and authentic with your responses.
9. **Pay attention to cues.** Actively monitor the other person's verbal cues and body language. If appearing uncomfortable or disinterested, wrap up the conversation in a polite way.
10. **Be open and authentic.** Be your true genuine self. People like sincerity.

Now that you know what to do, it is time for you to practice and make a new friend. You can confidently approach someone new, create a positive first impression, and set the stage for a pleasant conversation. There are numerous options for where and how you can meet potential new compatible friends:

Clubs and hobby groups: Join social clubs or organizations related to your interests, such as book clubs or cooking classes. These are great places to meet like-minded people and bond over shared passions.

Community events: Attend local events, festivals, concerts, fairs, or charity fundraisers to interact with people in your community. Eventbrite.com lists events for most communities.

Meetup groups: Websites like Meetup.com allow you to find and join groups based on activities or shared interests. You will find a wide range of activities such as photography, hiking, social change movements, and foreign language practice partners.

Volunteering: Volunteer work for a cause you care about allows you to give back to your community while introducing you to others who share your values.

Classes or workshops: Enroll in classes or workshops to learn new skills. Through yoga, dancing, cooking, or painting, you can improve yourself while having fun meeting people in a no-pressure environment.

Religious or spiritual communities: For those who are religious, spiritual, or curious, attending events at a local church, mosque, synagogue, or meditation center can help you find others who share your beliefs and provide a sense of community.

Networking events: Attend professional networking events, seminars, and conferences related to your field of work or study to expand your professional network.

Online communities: Participate in online forums and social media groups related to your interests to connect with others who share your passions and possibly lead to offline friendships.

Public places: Strike up conversations with people at public places, parks, coffee shops, or libraries. Most probably won't lead to a friendship, but you increase the chances by being open to talking with new people and making connections.

Fitness or Playing sports: Attend group fitness classes or participate in a recreational sports league. These are fun, keep you in shape, and create an opportunity to bond with others in a healthy way.

Making friends will take time and effort. By actively seeking out social opportunities and being a good listener, you can increase your chances of forming lasting friendships. Be open, approachable, and genuinely interested in getting to know others.

Self-Care

The top-grossing non-pimped stripper I ever knew told me to set aside time for weekly massages, yoga, meditation, and take regular vacations away from work. I did not know how to do those things and was also trained not to as they would have interfered with my income potential. Maybe you can relate. Do not fall into the trap of believing that your beauty maintenance activities satisfy the self-care requirement. When I actively did sex work, I viewed getting hair extensions, false eyelashes, and my nails done as self-care. That might be true for a normal woman, but as a sex worker, those can be work necessities.

So, what is self-care? Real self-care is maintaining balance and overall well-being by taking care of your physical, emotional, and mental health to ensure that you can effectively manage the challenges of life. Here are some self-care practices to incorporate into your daily routine:

- Physical self-care: Prioritize your physical health by engaging in regular exercise, maintaining a balanced healthy diet, and getting enough sleep.
- Emotional self-care: It is important to acknowledge and process your emotions. Rather than suppressing or ignoring them, talk through your emotions with a therapist, close friend, or creatively express yourself through journaling and art.
- Mental self-care: Stimulate your mind to promote personal growth through reading, learning new skills, or participating in workshops or classes.
- Spiritual self-care: Figure out what your spiritual beliefs are and engage in practices that support your connection to something greater than yourself, such as spending time in nature, meditating, participating in a spiritual community, and prayer.

Self-care habits significantly impact your energy level, mood, and overall well-being. Incorporate daily self-care routines into your life to prevent your physical body from getting damaged and to stave off mental health issues. Everything falls apart eventually if you do not take care of yourself. Self-care does more than just take care of your physical and mental health, it also preserves your job, your relationships, and everything else in your life.

As the airplane warning says, "when traveling with small children, always apply your own oxygen mask first," the same applies for other aspects of life. You cannot properly take care of other important things if you do not take care of yourself first. Get sufficient sleep, eat healthy, and spend time doing things you enjoy. It pays off in happiness, improved mood, energy level, and efficiency. One of the 10 Commandments even orders us to set aside time for rest. There is a reason. We function at our best this way.

On the topic of God, what are your religious or spiritual views? Studies show that people who have faith generally live an extra 4-10 years longer and are happier than those without. Take time to explore your beliefs and engage in practices that support your connection to something greater than yourself. Prayer reduces fear, stress, and loneliness. Gratitude has been shown to improve mental health, increase immunity, reduce pain, and improve sleep. All of these benefits have been demonstrated in repeatable peer-reviewed studies. If you have not thought this through much, ask yourself "why not?" Having faith and participating in spiritual practices are self-care.

Be patient with yourself as you incorporate these routines into your daily life. Your goal is to build self-care into a lifelong commitment. Through consistently prioritizing your physical and mental well-being, you create a more balanced, fulfilling life that supports your overall health and happiness.

Integrating work, relationships, and self-care

Integrate work, relationships, and self-care in a manageable way. Here are some strategies for achieving this integration:

- **Prioritize what matters most.** Reflect on what is most important to you and focus your time and energy in these areas. This might include prioritizing your health, personal relationships, or professional growth. By concentrating on what truly matters, you

will create a more balanced and fulfilling life.
- **Schedule self-care.** Treat self-care as a non-negotiable part of your routine, just as important as work or social commitments. Block out time in your schedule for activities that nourish your mind, body, and spirit. Make a conscious effort to stick to these plans.
- **Cultivate mindfulness.** Practicing mindfulness can help you stay present and focused on the task at hand, work, spending time with loved ones, or engaging in self-care. This greater focus leads to satisfaction and fulfillment in all areas of your life.
- **Be adaptable and flexible.** Life is full of surprises and changes, so it's important to remain flexible to adjusting your plans as needed. This means occasionally re-evaluating your priorities or making changes to your schedule to maintain balance.
- **Build a support network.** Surround yourself with people who understand and support your goals and values. These individuals can provide encouragement and guidance as you navigate the challenges of balancing work, relationships, and self-care.

A well-balanced life will allow you to thrive both with personal relationships and professionally within your career. One helpful approach for maintaining balance is to regularly assess and reevaluate your priorities. If you do not do this, you risk becoming stagnant and one day waking up not even being sure who you are and realizing that you are unhappy with your life. As your circumstances change, your priorities might also shift. By being honest with yourself about what is most important to you, you can alter course to stay true to yourself and pursue your passions. Don't fall asleep at the wheel of life.

Finally, no matter how hard you try, you can not always be perfect. There will be times where you do not reach your goals and may even outright fail. This is part of life. And some days will be busier or better than others. Do not permit yourself to be discouraged by the moments of uncertainty; they are opportunities for growth. Expect setbacks to happen. Remind yourself that self-compassion and maintaining balance is self-care.

CHAPTER 11
Legal

Understanding legal considerations is important for everyone, but it can be especially crucial for former sex workers. Laws and regulations surrounding sex work can vary greatly depending on where you live. Familiarizing yourself with these laws helps you to avoid any potential legal issues and ensure that you are aware of your rights.

While I am not a legal expert, I want to provide a little general information about how a prostitution conviction can potentially affect future employment in the United States. Of course, the impact of a conviction on your employment will depend upon the jurisdiction, what exactly you were convicted of, the specific job you are applying for, and the employer's policies.

Some occupations that could be completely barred or impacted by a prostitution conviction include:

1) <u>Legal professionals</u>: Attorneys and other legal professionals are subject to background checks and character assessments, and a prostitution conviction could be a disqualifying factor.
2) <u>Law enforcement</u>: Many police departments and other law enforcement agencies will disqualify applicants with a criminal history, including prostitution convictions.
3) <u>Government jobs</u>: Some federal, state, and local government positions require background checks and may exclude applicants with certain criminal records.
4) <u>Social workers and counselors</u>: These professionals need a license to practice, and a prostitution conviction may be a disqualifier per the specific licensing board's regulations.
5) <u>Healthcare professions</u>: Physicians, nurses, pharmacists, and other healthcare professionals may be required to

undergo background checks and may be rejected for having certain criminal convictions.
6) <u>Financial sector</u>: Jobs in banking, finance, and related industries that require background checks may eliminate applicants who have a prostitution conviction.
7) <u>Education professionals</u>: Teachers, school administrators, and other education professionals may also be subject to background checks, and a prostitution conviction could be a disqualifying factor.
8) <u>Childcare providers</u>: Individuals working in childcare or seeking a childcare provider license may be disqualified based on a criminal history, including prostitution convictions.
9) <u>Real estate agents and brokers</u>: Many states require background checks for real estate professionals, and a prostitution conviction could be a disqualifying factor.
10) <u>Licensed professions</u>: Certain professions that require licenses or certifications may have regulations that disqualify individuals with a criminal history, including prostitution convictions.

Expungement and arrest relief

If you have a criminal record related to your time in the sex industry, you may want to consider looking into expungement or sealing of your record. Expungement is a legal process in which the courts erase or seal your criminal conviction, effectively removing it from public view so that it no longer shows up on background checks. This can eliminate barriers when searching for employment, housing, or educational opportunities. Once you have had your arrest expunged, you can legally say that you were not arrested. If your criminal record is findable online, after your expungement has been approved you can demand those sites to update your information and remove the arrest record.

If you have past criminal charges, expungement might provide you with a fresh start toward gainful employment, housing, and other opportunities that you cannot qualify for with a criminal record. Expungement laws and eligibility requirements vary widely between jurisdictions.

Whether you are eligible for expungement is often based on:
- Type of offense: Some jurisdictions only allow for the expungement of nonviolent or misdemeanor convictions. More serious offenses, like violent crimes or sexual offenses, may not be eligible for expungement.
- Time since the conviction: Many jurisdictions require a waiting period after the completion of the sentence, during which you must remain crime-free. This waiting period can range from a few years to several decades, depending on the jurisdiction and the offense.
- Age at the time of the offense: In some cases, expungement may be more accessible for individuals who were minors at the time of the offense.
- Completion of sentence: To be eligible for expungement, the individual must typically complete all terms of their sentence, including probation, community service, and payment of fines or restitution.
- No pending charges or convictions: Most jurisdictions require that the individual seeking expungement has no pending criminal charges or subsequent convictions.

Some states have more lenient expungement laws, while others have more restrictive ones. Additionally, expungement may not be available for federal offenses.

Expungement and arrest relief are two separate legal processes that serve to limit the negative consequences of having a criminal record. Usually people need expungement, but sometimes there is only an arrest without conviction that causes shame or they want removed for some reason—and that is when arrest relief comes into play. While both aim to help individuals move past their criminal history, they differ in terms of scope and the stage of the criminal justice process addressed. I will recap expungement and then contrast it with arrest relief.

Expungement: Expungement is a legal process that can seal or erase your criminal record, effectively removing it from public view. A wide range of conviction offenses can be expunged. Once a record is expunged, it is as if the conviction never occurred, and you are no longer required to disclose, including when applying for most jobs or housing.

Arrest Relief: Arrest relief (sometimes referred to as "arrest record sealing" or "non-conviction record sealing") is a legal process specifically for arrest records. The purpose of arrest relief is to prevent you from suffering negative consequences from an arrest that did not end with a conviction. This often occurs in cases that are dismissed. Arrest relief seals the arrest record so that it is no longer accessible to the public or removes it from databases used for background checks.

While both expungement and arrest relief reduce the negative impact of your criminal record, they differ in the criminal justice processes they address and the records they apply to. Expungement pertains to convictions, whereas arrest relief focuses on arrests that did not result in convictions. It is important to note that the availability and eligibility criteria for expungement and arrest relief vary depending on the jurisdiction.

If you have a prostitution conviction or other prior arrest that concerns you, you can consult with a legal professional familiar with the laws within your jurisdiction to discuss your specific situation and options.

It is not cheap to hire attorneys for these processes. I personally hired an attorney to ensure that all of my necessary paperwork was completed correctly and filed, but it was expensive to pay to have it done for me. If money is not as easy to come by anymore and you have the time and motivation to do this yourself, you often can. Should you decide to pursue expungement without an attorney, this is how to do it yourself:

1) Research your jurisdiction's expungement and arrest relief laws to determine the specific process you must

follow.
2) Your criminal record can typically be obtained from the law enforcement agency that arrested you or the court where your case was handled. You must have a copy before applying for expungement or arrest relief.
3) Complete the necessary expungement or arrest relief forms. Some states may have online resources or self-help centers to assist you in completing the necessary paperwork.
4) File all of the necessary completed forms with the appropriate court. Usually there are filing fees, but fee waivers may be available for those who cannot afford to pay.
5) You will need to attend the hearing and present your case to the judge, explaining why you believe your record should be expunged or sealed.
6) After your expungement or arrest relief is granted, make sure you follow-up with law enforcement agencies and background check companies to ensure that your record was indeed updated and is no longer publicly available.

So, while it is possible to pursue expungement or arrest relief without an attorney, the process can be complex and time-consuming. If you are not comfortable navigating the legal system, or if your case has unique circumstances, it may be beneficial to consult with an attorney who can guide you through the process and ensure that all requirements are met.

Moving on

Be honest about your work history without disclosing unnecessary information on job applications. You do not need to provide explicit details about your past, just ensure that you are being truthful about your experience to help avoid potential issues down the line. Often strippers and escorts list their past occupations as "consultant," "sales," "customer service," and "entertainer."

Most jurisdictions have laws that protect people from discrimination based on race, religion, and sexual orientation. Although these protections do not explicitly cover former sex work, you may still be able to seek legal recourse if you believe you have been unfairly treated. Being aware of tenant rights and housing laws is also important. In some cases, landlords are permitted to discriminate against potential tenants due to their past work history. Familiarize yourself with local housing laws and tenant protections to ensure that you are treated fairly when searching for a new home. It is crucial to know your rights.

If you have personal information or images related to your time in the sex industry still available online, you may want to take steps to remove or protect this content. If you signed model releases, you will not be able to get those images down. However, if you did not, you can reach out directly to websites and platforms to request removal of your personal images or information. If you have the finances to do so, you might also consider working with an online reputation management service.

If you have outstanding debts or tax obligations related to your time in the sex industry, it is important to take care of them. You can speak with a financial advisor or tax professional to develop a plan for resolving outstanding debts in order to protect your financial future. Sometimes filing for bankruptcy is the correct choice. Take your current income to debt ratio into consideration and be aware that most bankruptcy courts will not forgive student loan debt.

Never hesitate to reach out for legal assistance. Many organizations offer free or low-cost legal services, and many jurisdictions have additional assistance for human and sexual trafficking survivors. These organizations do care and at least will provide emotional support if you are being shunned by everyone else. Do not be afraid to ask for help; you do not have to hide. Understanding your rights and protecting yourself legally can be an essential part of your transition. Yes, navigating legal considerations is complex, but staying informed and seeking professional guidance can make all the difference. You have rights and deserve to be treated fairly. Remember you are worthy, even if you are not being treated as such.

Family law

When it comes to family law matters, former sex workers face unique and uncomfortable challenges, especially in cases involving child custody or divorce. Always tell your attorney about your past. It should be one of the first things you say. If you are going through a family law case, you can be sure that your ex will likely out you to hurt your side of the case; make sure you disclose first so that your attorney will not be caught off guard. It is essential to collaborate with an attorney who understands your specific situation and can advocate for your rights and best interests.

Pay attention to how your attorney reacts to your past. Your attorney should respond to you, file your documents and evidence, respond to calls and emails, respect you in words and action, and represent you the way that you ask. Be aware that attorneys are people, and sometimes people allow their own personal prejudice or bias to negatively affect or influence their professionalism. Hopefully that will not be your experience, but in case it is, immediately fire any attorney who is incompetent or does not represent you in the way that you need. You do not deserve an attorney who charges full fees yet won't put in the effort to do a proper job. If your attorney does not provide proper representation, research the Bar laws for your state and file an official complaint if they were not followed.

I have had personal experience with family court, and it was not pretty. Instead of focusing on the issue of what was best for the child, everyone stayed focused on my past—including my own attorney. At this stage, I had not done sex work in almost a decade and had completely changed my life. Sex work is interesting, people want to stay focused on it and shaming people on the stand is tolerated, if not normal. Your attorney should step in here if it is not relevant to your case. Mine did not. What I tried to do and probably should have been more vocal about was to insist that my past was my past and I am now a new creation in Christ (true for me). I did not say those words and I regret it. I was judged as if still guilty today, as if I had just given a blow job around the corner with no consideration for how much my life had changed, how much time had passed since, or even that I had been managed back then. Court officials asked me sexually detailed questions about things that had happened years earlier, that in no way related to our family law situation. You should be forewarned that you will likely be asked irrelevant questions because people are curious and taboo pasts are often interesting to others.

I was completely honest, yet I was then directly told that I was an uncredible witness and a liar. Just as my pimp always told me would happen... It felt like a nightmare. I still believe that being honest is the correct thing to do and I am glad that I was, although I now understand why so many people are not. Even though you are honest, people will still often assume you are lying and judge you it. They may assume guilt instead of innocence and then proactively look for anything that seems off. This means if you need time to think, do not remember something, or have PTSD or dyslexia that causes a comprehension delay, that might be proof in their eyes against you. Hopefully you have a competent attorney who will point those things out. Being caught lying is a risk, but sadly being accused and punished for lying when you are honest carries the same punishment. This is one of the realities of having a past: many people will refuse to look beyond it. This is them, not you, but it hurts you.

Think through whether you want your past brought up or not. Maybe you will not have a choice because someone else will introduce it into your case. Maybe it is within your power to choose. I had the choice to keep this secret, but I truly felt that how my past related to the other person in the case was important background information. Do you think your judge will look at the current reality or condemn you for what you used to do? Is there any way to know this before you choose to be honest or are outed? Make sure your attorney sets aside time to roleplay with you in advance so you can be prepared and know how to react in court when questioned. All attorneys should do that…so, if your attorney does not, that is another red flag. Mine did not do that, and it was disastrous.

CHAPTER 12
Physical and mental health

Leaving the sex industry can be physically and mentally triggering. After leaving, it is common to experience a range of emotions including anxiety, depression, shame, and guilt. Therefore, it is key to pay attention to prioritizing your well-being and seek professional help. Mental health professionals are trained to help you work through emotional difficulties. If you need more than talk therapy, psychiatrists can prescribe psychiatric medication. There are many organizations which provide free or low-cost mental health services for trauma survivors, including those who have worked in the sex industry.

Incorporating regular exercise into your routine helps improve both your physical and mental health. You can run, walk, weightlift, do yoga, join a gym or participate in classes. Exercise is great for your physical health and has also been shown to elevate mood, reduce stress and anxiety, increase energy levels, and improve sleep quality. Consider developing a bedtime routine to help you wind down before bed: read a book, take a bath, or meditate. If you look at your phone, computer, or TV at night, consider using blue light glasses. Blue light zaps melatonin (the natural sleep hormone) from your system which directly interferes with your sleep quality; blue light glasses protect you from that. If cost is a concern, you can purchase a pair for $1.25 at Dollar Tree. Ideally, you should keep a steady sleep and wake schedule. Wake up each day without an alarm if that is possible for you. Ensure that the room you sleep in is as dark as possible and your mattress is comfortable. All of these tips will help you sleep better and wake well-rested.

Nutrition

Most nutritionists teach you to begin your day with a nutritious breakfast to provide you with energy to start your day. However, different people have differing ideas for what defines healthy eating. Since I am not a nutritionist, rather than giving advice on what you should eat or promoting one diet over the other, I will detail the most commonly accepted diets that have been considered healthy by large populations. You can read them for yourself and then decide which resonates best for you.

<u>The Food Pyramid</u>: The United States Department of Agriculture (USDA) developed the Food Pyramid in 1992, and for years it was the standard taught in schools for healthy nutrition. The food groups were put into a visual hierarchy that recommended how many servings from each food group people should eat each day. Just as pyramids are wider at the bottom with a significantly smaller tip, people were encouraged to eat more foods from the base of the pyramid and almost none near the top. The Food Pyramid was divided into six tiers:

Sparingly, or use very little: fats, oils, and sweets

2-3 servings per day: protein (meat, poultry, fish, dry beans, eggs, and nuts)

2-3 servings per day: dairy (milk, yogurt, and cheese)

2-4 servings per day: fruits

3-5 servings per day: vegetables

6-11 servings per day: grains (bread, cereal, rice, and pasta)

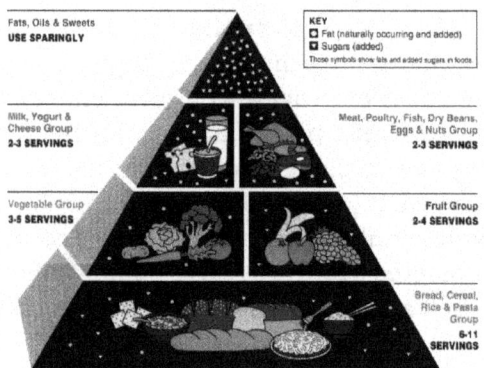

As you can see, the Food Pyramid encouraged individuals to consume more grains, fruits, and vegetables, while limiting the intake of fats, oils, and sweets. The Food Pyramid was criticized for its failure to differentiate between whole versus refined grains and sugars, and healthy fats; that oversight was considered a possible contributor toward the rise in chronic diseases and obesity.

MyPlate: With updated research, MyPlate replaced the Food Pyramid. It was designed to be an updated visual representation for balanced eating. MyPlate depicts a plate divided into four sections, with fruits, vegetables, grains, and proteins each occupying a portion of the plate and a small circle nearby to allow for limited dairy. Vegetables and fruits comprise half of the plate, with proteins and grains making up the other half. MyPlate is a straightforward method of emphasizing portion control and balanced meal composition.

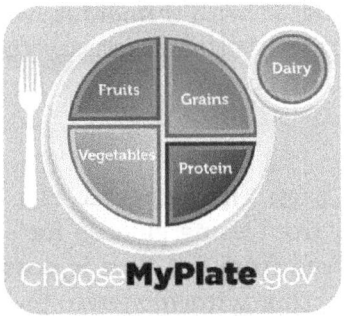

The Mediterranean Diet: The Mediterranean diet emphasizes a high intake of fruits, vegetables, whole grains, and legumes, along with healthy fats from olive oil and fish. Dairy products, poultry, and eggs are consumed in moderation, while red meat and processed foods are limited. It further categorizes healthier fat sources and encourages whole grains over refined. Research has shown that the Mediterranean diet promotes weight loss and longevity while reducing the risk of type 2 diabetes, stroke, and heart disease.

The Paleo Diet: The Paleo diet eliminates dairy, grains, and legumes completely and instead focuses on fish, lean meats, vegetables, fruits, nuts, and seeds. Proponents of the Paleo diet argue that it reduces inflammation and improves digestion, while critics point out that the omission of certain food groups may lead to nutrient deficiencies and an unsustainable diet for the environment and long-term health.

The Vegan Diet: Vegetarian signifies no meat, but vegan takes that a step further by eliminating all animal-derived foods, meat, dairy, and eggs. Permitted foods are whole grains, vegetables, legumes, fruits, plant-based protein, nuts, and seeds. The vegan diet is considered more environmentally sustainable and has been associated with numerous health benefits. That said, supplementation is often necessary to receive sufficient essential nutrients and protein.

The Ketogenic Diet: The ketogenic diet aims to shift the body's metabolism from using glucose for energy to utilizing ketone bodies derived from fat. This is possible through very low-carbohydrate eating with moderate-protein and high-fat. This diet emphasizes the consumption of meat, poultry, fish, dairy, nuts, seeds, and non-starchy vegetables, while severely limiting grains, fruits, legumes, and sugar. The ketogenic diet contrasts with MyPlate's recommendations, particularly regarding the proportion of carbohydrates and fats. While some studies suggest that the ketogenic diet may promote weight loss and improve blood sugar control, critics argue that its long-term effects on overall health are unclear and that it may be challenging to sustain.

The Raw Food Diet: The raw food diet aims to preserve the natural enzymes and nutrients in foods that are often destroyed during cooking. It is based on the principle of consuming unprocessed, uncooked, and primarily plant-based foods, such as sprouted grains and legumes, vegetables, nuts, seeds, and fruits. The raw food diet has been associated with weight loss, improved digestion, and increased energy. However, critics argue that a strict raw food diet can lead to nutrient deficiencies, particularly in vitamin B12, calcium, and iron, and even claim that some foods are more nutritious or safer to eat when cooked.

In conclusion, MyPlate serves as a general basic guideline for balanced eating, while the Mediterranean, Paleo, vegan, ketogenic, and raw food diets each offer more specialized approaches to healthy eating habits. The Mediterranean diet closely aligns with MyPlate, but with a stronger emphasis on whole foods and healthy fats. The Paleo, vegan, ketogenic, and raw food diets deviate from MyPlate in that they actually eliminate or modify certain food groups, presenting unique benefits and challenges. Ultimately, the most effective diet for you will depend on your specific health needs, preferences, and lifestyle. Prioritizing moderation, variety, and whole foods is key to achieving optimal health and well-being.

No matter which diet you decide upon for you, it is crucial to stay hydrated by drinking enough water each day. Proper hydration is essential for maintaining bodily functions, improving digestion, and enhancing cognitive function. Harvard University recommends a minimum of 4-6 cups of water per day. Keep a water bottle with you and sip regularly to ensure you get the recommended daily intake. While most people do not put themselves at risk of this, be aware that drinking excessive amounts of water can also hurt your health, and how much that is will depend upon many factors, so pay attention to your body.

A lot of mental health problems are tied to vitamin deficiencies—most notably with B-vitamin deficiencies—so taking a good multivitamin is a great idea. If finances are tight, food banks, local community gardens, and the discount sales in the produce department (on Mondays where I live) allow you to continue eating healthy foods to avoid deficiencies. Alcohol and drugs can hurt your mental and physical health; abstinence is best although, if that is not something you can do right now, lowered use (called "harm reduction") is better than no change.

Eating disorders

Do you have disordered eating? Do you either eat extraordinarily little, binge eat, exercise excessively, or purge? You are not alone in this. Eating disorders are extremely common among sex workers for a few distinct reasons.

An overwhelming majority of sex workers have experienced childhood trauma. Research shows a strong correlation between early traumatic experiences and the development of eating disorders. Peer-reviewed research reveals that over 60% of those with eating disorders have also experienced trauma. If you were neglected, a victim of physical or sexual abuse, witnessed violence, or had a loved one die when you were young, all of these traumas could have disrupted your early sense of safety and control. Trauma often has a lasting impact that can directly lead to eating disorder coping mechanism behaviors to regain a sense of control or find relief from emotional pain. In addition to early life traumas, you have also been at a higher risk for experiencing trauma due to the nature of sex work.

Eating disorders are complex and influenced by a mix of genetic, environmental, and psychological factors. By acknowledging the connection between your past trauma and your eating disorder, you can work towards understanding the underlying issues and find the most effective path to recovery. Eating disorders can have severe consequences on both physical and psychological health. While trauma is often a contributing factor, it is not the only possible cause of disordered eating.

Two other factors also increase the likelihood of sex workers having eating disorders. The first is the body image pressures of the sex industry. The adult industry places a strong emphasis on physical appearance which pressures workers to maintain unrealistic beauty standards and a certain body type or weight. In order to conform to such stringent body ideals, you might adapt disordered eating patterns. A second potential influencer is substance use disorders. Sex workers have a higher rate of substance use due to the nature of the work. Substance use can exacerbate or contribute to the development of disordered eating behaviors while also increasing the risk of experiencing additional trauma.

Eating disorders are normalized and even viewed as a positive trait for adult industry workers. It has taken me a lot of years to heal half of my body image issues since leaving the sex industry. I do not know if I will ever be able to look at myself through a normal lens. All abnormal eating habits and distorted attitudes towards body weight, shape, and appearance usually fit somewhere under the eating disorder umbrella.

Anorexia Nervosa. If you have a distorted body image, an intense fear of gaining weight, and persistently try to lose weight even when you are already underweight, you may have anorexia nervosa. You restrict your food intake, engage in excessive exercise, take drugs that are known to cause people to lose weight, or use other weight loss methods such as purging, fasting, or using laxatives.

Signs that you may have anorexia nervosa include:
- Significant weight loss without any medical explanation
- Obsession with weight, body shape, and appearance
- Fear of gaining weight, even when underweight
- Distorted body image
- Denial of the seriousness of low body weight
- Avoidance of social situations involving food
- Intense, excessive exercise

Bulimia Nervosa. If you have recurrent episodes of binge eating followed by compensatory behaviors to prevent weight gain, force yourself to vomit, spend excessive time in saunas, take drugs to lose weight, misuse laxatives, excessively exercise, or fast, you may have bulimia nervosa. You feel a lack of control during binge-eating episodes and experience guilt or shame afterwards.

Signs that you may have bulimia nervosa include:
- Recurrent episodes of binge eating, characterized by eating copious amounts of food in a short period and feeling a lack of control
- Regular use of compensatory behaviors, such as self-induced vomiting, misuse of laxatives, excessive exercise, or fasting
- Preoccupation with weight, body shape, and appearance
- Feelings of guilt, shame, or distress after binge eating

- Normal or fluctuating body weight

Binge Eating Disorder. If you have recurrent episodes of binge eating without the use of compensatory behaviors to prevent weight gain, you may have binge eating disorder. You feel a lack of control during binge episodes and experience feelings of guilt, shame, or distress afterwards.
Signs that you may have binge eating disorder include:
- Recurrent episodes of binge eating, characterized by eating copious amounts of food in a short period and feeling a lack of control
- Eating rapidly, until uncomfortably full, or when not physically hungry
- Eating alone or in secret due to embarrassment
- Feelings of guilt, shame, or distress after binge eating
- Possible weight gain or obesity

Body Dysmorphic Disorder (BDD). While not necessarily an eating disorder, both anorexia nervosa and bulimia nervosa can coexist with body dysmorphic disorder. BDD is characterized by becoming excessively preoccupied with perceived flaws or defects in your physical appearance. Your perceived imperfections are often minor or not noticeable to others, but when you have BDD, they cause you significant distress and can interfere with your daily functioning.

You might find yourself engaging in repetitive behaviors, constantly checking yourself in the mirror, obsessing over grooming, skin picking, or frequently seeking reassurance from others about your appearance. You experience significant distress and anxiety related to your perceived imperfections which can lead to social isolation, depression, and low self-esteem. It can be difficult to concentrate on tasks or maintain relationships due to your constant preoccupation with your appearance. You might avoid social situations or public places for fear of being judged or scrutinized by others or spend excessive amounts of time getting ready. It is not uncommon to be addicted to plastic surgery procedures and treatments to "fix" your perceived flaws, often with little satisfaction.

Body dysmorphic disorder is a mental health disorder, not simply self-absorption or vanity. While there does not appear to be much research into whether BDD is correlated with the sex industry, those of us who have worked in that industry know that it runs rampant. If you did not have BDD before entering sex work, it is hard to work in that industry without developing that or other self-esteem issues due to the body image pressures.

I will self-disclose that I struggled with body dysmorphic disorder for 20 years. I cannot count how many procedures I have done which includes cosmetic surgeries, injectables, lasers, and non-invasive treatments. I used to joke that I was the closest most people would ever come to meeting Joan Rivers. I say that with the utmost of respect, I even bought her excellent book about cosmetic surgery: "Men Are Stupid...And They Like Big Boobs: A Woman's Guide to Beauty Through Plastic Surgery." I now realize how weird multiple procedures must seem to normal people, but at the time and within my circle it was normal. My friends and I all had direct phone numbers to top cosmetic surgeons on our cell phones and sometimes were such frequent clients that we received discounts. You may not be to this extreme, yet I self-disclose here because you certainly knew people like this and will now easily be able to identify this condition for what it is.

Just to wrap up, eating disorders and body dysmorphic disorder are common, socially acceptable and respected conditions among the adult industry. All of them have a high correlation to trauma and substance use, too. These are immensely common problems to have as you are leaving the industry, you are not alone, and help is available. Identifying whether you fit the signs and symptoms is the first step towards seeking help and support. If you do, you can consult with a healthcare professional for proper assessment, diagnosis, and treatment. The earlier the intervention and support, the greater your chances of recovery. Treatment options for BDD include cognitive-behavioral therapy (CBT), trauma treatments, medication, or a combination of all of these, depending on your severity and specific needs.

How to know if you are a good weight

When you have had a past history of body image distortion and external social pressures, it can be challenging to determine the accuracy of your current body image. This is something that I still struggle with myself. Other people may say you look fine, but after so long of needing to look a certain way, you are probably much harder on yourself than anyone else would be. And it may be subconscious.

One effective way to determine if your thoughts are reasonable or not is to track yourself and keep a log. Scales can lie due to water weight fluctuations. Therefore, measurements are often a better determiner. If you frequently measure yourself and write down the results, you will see the normal patterns for your body, how it changes during distinct parts of your cycle, and by how much. After 6 months of tracking, you will have an external tool you can compare yourself to if you are unsure when your current assessment of your body is accurate. Another way to judge your body is by how well your clothes fit. When people first start lifting weights, their weight goes up, but their clothes get looser. This is because muscle weighs more than fat. The tape measure might catch this too, whereas a scale can hurt your self-esteem.

Are your expectations for how you think you should look based on how the average person of your age actually looks? Are your expectations based on how you previously looked? Could they be from social media, television, or print advertisements? Or are you comparing yourself to people within the sex industry? It is important to watch out for beauty standards that are unrealistic for the average person. Even if you looked a certain way in the past, you were younger in the past and there might be other factors at play, too. Be kind to yourself and remind yourself that a fluctuating body image is normal. Lots of models have severe self-esteem issues, and the world looks at them in awe for how perfect they are. Consciously evaluate whether you are being much harder on yourself than is reasonable; if you are unable, you ask others who understand healthy body image what their opinions are.

Instead of concentrating on appearance, focus on how well your body functions. Are you strong? Are you flexible? Do you tire out easily? Move your body in ways that make you feel good about yourself. Yoga, dance, lift weights if that's your thing. Set physical goals based on functionality and health instead of perception in the mirror.

You will probably find that people outside of the industry are much more accepting of whatever body you have than people still in. So, surround yourself with new people who appreciate you for who you are on the inside. Build a support network of those uplifting people. Once most of your social circle no longer judges you, it will be much more obvious when you judge yourself. This is not picking a group of "yes men" to lie to you or make you feel better, but instead choosing regular people who are outside of the distorted normal that exists within the sex industry's unrealistic expectations.

Along those lines, if you cannot stop obsessing over your body image, consider seeing a therapist. Therapists who specialize in body image issues can help you to recognize if your beliefs are accurate or false. They can also help you to identify the factors influencing your perceptions and teach you how to develop a healthier and more accurate body image. Keeping a journal of your weight, measurements, food intake and thoughts, and then sharing those written notes with your therapist can be helpful, too.

Other things that will help with your body image are general self-care. Make sure you are getting enough sleep, you are eating healthily, and you are minimizing stress in your life. In addition to self-care being important for your mental health, without self-care your body can undesirably go up or down in weight and lose definition. Not monitoring your stress level, quality of sleep, or the nutritiousness of your diet can cause the condition of your skin to worsen, make you become "flabby," age your appearance, and thin your hair. That is fine for someone who does not care about those things...but, assuming you do, remain aware. Depression or stressing often causes people to neglect the non-appearance side of self-care, and that neglect can directly cause physical appearance side effects.

Affirmations are also helpful. This one is hard for lots of people, especially when they do not believe what is being said in the affirmation. Let me explain. When you purposefully and consciously choose to say loving things aloud to yourself, you positively reprogram your brain. Within our own minds, we just think. But, when you say affirmations while standing in front of a mirror, you are thinking, saying, hearing, and seeing the words and absorb them in 4 different ways. We sometimes believe others when "we should have known better" because we absorb more of their words than our own. Even when you do not feel it is completely true, doing positive affirmations will help your mental health and body image.

"My body is healthy."
"My body is fine for my current lifestyle."
"I love myself."

Yes, it may feel like a lie. Yet, if other people outside of that industry tell you that your current thinking is dysfunctional then it is important to do affirmations to create a whole new belief system. The adult industry often brainwashes people into having unhealthy body image standards. Affirmations build self-esteem.

Now, I will go over those affirmations again and how to respond to them if you believe they are lies.

- *"My body is healthy."* - If you do not believe this, create a physical routine by lifting weights, doing cardio, or doing both. Also, clean up your diet. A healthy body is made up of proper exercise and nutrition. And finally, make sure you are sleeping enough because a lack of sleep can cause your body to not function or recover as well as it should. Do not drink alcohol or do drugs; if this one is a challenge for you, seek help.

- *"My body is fine for my current lifestyle."* - If you do not believe this, why not? The list above will tell you how to fix your body if it is not healthy. Fix your health if needed. However, if all of those things are in place already, you are most likely judging yourself against a beauty ideal instead of being realistic about whether your body is fine for your lifestyle. Recognize that disconnect.
- *"I love myself."* - This is a hard one because often we do not realize when we have hateful behaviors towards ourselves. When you say this one, does it feel false? Not loving and respecting yourself can lead to all sorts of problems, addictions, false thoughts, and drama in your life. If this one feels uncomfortable or if you have to add qualifiers to the end of the sentence to make it feel true for you, you should seek therapy. You have a deep hurt and healing it will help many aspects of your life, not just your body image.

While using your new affirmations, remain mindful and self-aware. Look at yourself in the mirror as you speak. Make eye contact with yourself and soften your eyes to reflect love. Affirmations are an act of love. You are reassuring yourself and that is self-love. Self-love is new to many. If you had a childhood where you did not get enough love, if you have an unhealthy attachment style, if you have been the victim of narcissistic abuse, or if you have worked in a degrading occupation, self-love goes out the window. Healthy people do love themselves. Self-love does not mean self-absorption or narcissism; self-love is self-respect and believing you are worthy.

Needing a psychiatrist

Eating disorders like anorexia, bulimia, and body dysmorphic disorder are all treatable mental health conditions. For some, talk therapy is enough; for others, medication may be necessary. Your treatment path will depend on how long it has been a problem and the underlying factors.

While occasional stress, sadness, or anxiety are common experiences, there are certain signs which indicate you need more than just a therapist and should seek psychiatric care. Therapists and psychologists generally focus on talk-therapy. In contrast, psychiatrists are medical doctors who primarily prescribe psychiatric medication. Depression and anxiety are among the top reasons people see psychiatrists. There are many different medications on the market to help you cope with persistent feelings of sadness, hopelessness, despair, or worry that interferes with your daily life. Even if you have an anti-medication mindset, sometimes prescriptions are the correct choice for a specific circumstance or as a stopgap to get you through. If you find yourself in a mental trench that you cannot pull yourself out of on your own, medications can help.

You have likely seen the commercials stating, "depression can include loss of interest in activities you once enjoyed, changes in appetite or sleep patterns, difficulty concentrating, and feelings of hopelessness, worthlessness or guilt." However, the symptom that people rarely think about is a feeling of apathy. Maybe you do not want to do normal things because it just does not seem to matter anymore. This might be depression since it does not always surface as extreme sadness. Although, if you ever struggle with thoughts of self-harm or suicide, then it becomes crucial to seek help immediately. A psychiatrist can assess your risk, provide support, and develop a treatment plan that will include medication to stabilize you as quickly as possible.

If you experience "losing time," you should also make an appointment with a psychiatrist. Non-substance-related blackouts or time seeming to pass much slower or much quicker than normal is often caused by treatable mental health conditions. Extreme mood swings, including difficulty managing aggression or anger, withdrawing from social situations, or engaging in impulsive or risky behaviors also warrant making an appointment. These changes are often indicative of underlying mental health issues that require professional attention and/or medical intervention.

Similarly, if you find yourself constantly worrying or feeling anxious to the point that it impacts your daily life, a psychiatrist can help. There is a huge difference between anxiety and stress. Stress is a lot of pressure or a list of things to do, and often that pressure relates directly to a deadline. Anxiety, on the other hand, is a constant underlying worry even when there is no deadline or direct pressure. You can have a to-do list of 100 things and have stress without anxiety and be able to cope fine. But with anxiety, a list of three things can seem insurmountable. For most people, stress is a short-term response to things happening in life, whereas anxiety can be a long-term mental health condition that interferes with your quality of life. Stress is just circumstantial, versus anxiety which is mental-health related and can be treated. When your symptoms become overwhelming, make you unhappy, and interfere with your ability to function, seek professional help.

For those who experience periods of extreme emotional highs and lows, these variations could be signs of bipolar disorder. Depressive episodes can make you feel disinterested in life, suicidal, apathetic, sad, or drained. Manic phases may make you feel irritable, impulsive, invincible, or overly energetic. Delusion and hallucination symptoms are indicative of a psychotic disorder. These conditions will significantly negatively impact your daily life. You deserve to be happy and stable. Make an appointment right away to speak with a mental health professional for specialized treatment.

Substance use is a common way to self-medicate underlying mental health issues. If you struggle with substance abuse or addiction, a psychiatrist may be able to help. Psychiatrists can prescribe medication to address both your addiction and any underlying mental health concerns.

Finally, if you have already tried to heal your mental health issues every other way—using self-help books, support groups, therapy, nutrition—and yet still find your symptoms won't go away or are getting worse, it is time to consult a psychiatrist. Medication management or more specialized therapeutic approaches are probably required for your recovery.

In conclusion, part of taking charge of your mental health is recognizing the signs when you need to see a psychiatrist and then being willing to do so. Be honest with yourself because you know if you are not okay. Thoughts of self-harm, depression, delusions, hallucinations, or other persistent symptoms that interfere with your daily life are all valid reasons schedule a psychiatrist appointment. Prioritizing your mental well-being is crucial for your future happiness.

Can I regulate with vitamins?

I am not a medical doctor, a psychiatrist, nor a nutritionist so I am unable to tell you what you should do. When it comes to myself, I do take vitamins to keep myself stable. That said, back when I felt my mental health needed additional help, I did seek out psychiatric help. Here is some basic information about how some vitamins affect mental health. I do recommend that you speak with a doctor instead of self-medicating on your own.

Vitamin deficiencies have been shown to exacerbate, contribute to, and even help heal some mental health conditions. While vitamins alone are generally not direct treatment for mental health disorders, addressing deficiencies can help alleviate symptoms or improve overall mental health. Some mental health conditions that may be influenced by vitamin deficiencies include:
    1. Depression: Deficiencies in vitamin D, B vitamins (particularly B1, B6, B9, and B12), and omega-3 fatty

acids have been linked to depression.
2. Anxiety: Low levels of B vitamins, vitamin D, and magnesium have been associated with anxiety.
3. Cognitive decline and dementia: Deficiencies in B vitamins, particularly B12, B6, and folate (B9), as well as vitamin D, have been linked to cognitive decline and an increased risk of dementia, including Alzheimer's disease.
4. Neuropsychiatric symptoms: Vitamin B3 and B12 deficiencies can lead to neuropsychiatric symptoms, including irritability, mood disturbances, and even psychosis in severe cases.
5. Attention deficit hyperactivity disorder (ADHD): Some research suggests that children with ADHD may have lower levels of certain nutrients, such as zinc, magnesium, and omega-3 fatty acids.
6. Schizophrenia: There has been some evidence to support that B3 (niacin) can be helpful in reducing symptoms. If you are specifically interested in this, I would direct you to research by Dr. Abram Hoffer who stated, "For schizophrenics, the natural recovery rate is 50 percent. With orthomolecular medicine, the recovery rate is 80 percent. With drugs, it is 10 percent. If you use just drugs, you won't get well." (Hoffer, Saul, & Foster. *Niacin: The Real Story.* 2nd *Ed.* Basic Health Publications, 2023.)

It is important to note that, while correcting vitamin deficiencies can be helpful in maintaining appropriate mental health, they are not a replacement for speaking with a medical professional. For many people, a comprehensive treatment approach that includes therapy, proper nutrition and medication is necessary to effectively manage mental health conditions.

CHAPTER 13
Sobriety

Drug and alcohol use within the sex work industry is considered normal and socially acceptable. I don't judge you if you used then or still are. I was there, too. Reasons for using vary greatly and are influenced by personal history, working conditions, and social pressures. As a coping mechanism, drugs and alcohol are common for dealing with stress, stigma, and the emotional challenges experienced with this kind of work. Liquid courage and drugs create artificial comfort and increase confidence when interacting with clients. Self-medicating in response to past or ongoing trauma, mental health issues, or other personal struggles is also common.

The adult industry atmosphere often contributes to substance use. Drugs abound and it is easy to find what you want. It is a party. As such, social pressures and expectations within the industry often play a role in encouraging drug and alcohol use. The normalization of substance use can make it difficult to abstain, seek help for addiction, or change occupations. Harm reduction is the concept of lessening use instead of quitting, and that can be a positive change or a steppingstone toward sobriety if complete sobriety is not your current goal. If sobriety is not important to you, skip to the next chapter.

Being honest with current friends and co-workers about your desire to get and stay sober and clearly stating your boundaries is crucial. Tell them it is important to you that they respect and support your decision. Ensure that they know you won't be participating in activities involving substance use, and you might leave certain situations if you feel uncomfortable or triggered. True friends will understand and not tempt you; they may even remind you of your goal when you are about to slip. Be mentally prepared to distance yourself from friends who refuse to be supportive of your sobriety or who keep putting you at risk of relapse.

Getting and staying sober when your friends use drugs or drink is tough. The adage, "One day at a time" applies. Identifying who you normally drink or use with, and the cause, are good first steps toward determining if it is habit, if your friends are triggers, or if you have a biological addiction. Some people need to find entirely new friends. To create a support network, look for sober friends or people who share your commitment to sobriety outside of your current friend group. There is always at least one sober person in every environment, you can find new friends through support groups, online forums, or even at local events within your community. Create a more balanced social life that does not revolve around substances with these new friends.

If using has been your default, you will need to learn how to cope with stress and manage your triggers in other ways. Common coping techniques include therapy, exercise, meditation, a healthy diet, and spending time with sober friends. How many of those are you currently doing? Learning how to manage triggers and cope with stress without turning to drugs or alcohol is essential. When hungry or sleepy, people make bad decisions, so pay extra attention to eating clean and getting sufficient rest. A therapist or coach can help you develop healthy coping strategies tailored to your specific needs.

Research has proven that having faith-based recovery is more effective than non-faith-based recovery. Addiction is inherently selfish, whereas faith-based recovery asserts that there is something outside of yourself with more power than you. It is important that the something greater than you is not another living person whom you value more than yourself. Inpatient and outpatient rehabilitation programs can both be effective if you have true determination to change your life.

The most well-known of the outpatient treatments are 12-

step programs like Alcoholics Anonymous (AA) or Narcotics Anonymous (NA). These programs are a great starting point and are social in nature, but they are also often court-mandated so there are many attendees who have not actually quit nor committed to sobriety. If that might make you relapse, you can also look into other similar programs like Celebrate Recovery.

Alcoholics Anonymous and Narcotics Anonymous are considered secular and refer to a "Higher Power." In contrast, Celebrate Recovery is a Christian-based recovery program and refers directly to God. 12-Step programs are free and can provide a sense of community and accountability as you connect with others who understand your struggles and are also working towards sobriety.

The 12 Steps of Addiction Recovery Programs

1. We admitted we were powerless over our addictions and compulsive behaviors, and that our lives had become unmanageable.
2. We came to believe that a power greater than ourselves could restore us to sanity.
3. We made a decision to turn our lives and our wills over to the care of God as we understood Him.
4. We made a searching and fearless moral inventory of ourselves.
5. We admitted to God, to ourselves, and to another human being the exact nature of our wrongs.
6. We were entirely ready to have God remove all these defects of character.
7. We humbly asked Him to remove our shortcomings.
8. We made a list of all persons we had harmed and became willing to make amends to them all.
9. We made direct amends to such people wherever possible, except when to do so would injure them or others.
10. We continued to take personal inventory, and when we were wrong, promptly admitted it.
11. We sought through prayer and meditation to improve our conscious contact with God as we understood Him, praying only for knowledge of His

will for us and the power to carry that out.
12. Having had a spiritual awakening as the result of these steps, we tried to carry this message to others and to practice these principles in all our affairs.

<u>These same steps in lay language:</u>

Step 1: Admit that you have a problem.

Step 2: Have faith that something greater than yourself can help you.

Step 3: Surrender your will to that same something greater identified in Step 2.

Step 4: Reflect on all your current and past relationships and make a comprehensive list of the emotions invoked within you for each relationship. Take special care to note any resentments, anger, jealousy, envy. This sounds easy, but people hold in many more negative emotions than they are consciously aware of.

Step 5: Admit aloud everything within the Step 4 list to a trusted third party who is not on the list. This will probably be someone from the group or a therapist. This step is truly crucial for healing addiction as these negative emotions are often catalysts for self-medication.

Step 6: Accept that you have these harbored toxic emotions and believe that the something greater than yourself defined in Step 2 will help you let go of them.

Step 7: Humbly ask the power greater than yourself defined in Step 2 to remove your harbored toxic emotions.

Step 8: Take responsibility for your own bad behavior by making a list of everyone you have harmed over the years.

Step 9: Genuinely apologize to everyone you listed in Step 8 unless contacting them can directly hurt them physically or emotionally (or could put yourself in danger).

Step 10: For the future, stay self-aware to live a lifestyle that includes Step 8 and Step 9 in your daily life.

Step 11: Deepen your personal connection to that which you

defined in Step 2 as greater than yourself.
Step 12: Give back to the group by being there as support for the new people who need your help and guidance.

When Alcoholics Anonymous first began, it was a Christian-based group. However, over the years the terminology changed to accommodate people of all faiths. God was changed to Higher Power. The Anonymous groups work well for atheists who frequently consider the collective group their higher power, agnostics, and also people of other faiths. If you are a Christian, a Christian group may be a better fit.

Celebrate Recovery is a Jesus-centered, 12-step recovery program. It is similar to the Anonymous groups yet more Biblically-based and the verbiage explicitly defines the higher power. This program creates a faith-based supportive community for participants to spiritually and emotionally grow while getting sober.

<u>How Scriptural verses directly relate to each of the 12 Steps</u>
1. We admitted we were powerless over our addictions and compulsive behaviors, that our lives had become unmanageable.
   "I know that nothing good lives in me, that is, in my sinful nature. For I have the desire to do what is good, but I cannot carry it out." - Romans 7:18 (NIV)
2. We came to believe that a power greater than ourselves could restore us to sanity.
   "For it is God who works in you to will and to act according to his good purpose." - Philippians 2:13 (NIV)
3. We made a decision to turn our lives and our wills over to the care of God.
   "Therefore, I urge you, brothers, in view of God's mercy, to offer your bodies as living sacrifices, holy and pleasing to God

- this is your spiritual act of worship." - Romans 12:1 (NIV)

4. We made a searching and fearless moral inventory of ourselves.

"Let us examine our ways and test them, and let us return to the Lord." - Lamentations 3:40 (NIV)

5. We admitted to God, to ourselves, and to another human being the exact nature of our wrongs.

"Therefore, confess your sins to each other and pray for each other so that you may be healed." - James 5:16 (NIV)

6. We were entirely ready to have God remove all these defects of character.

"Humble yourselves before the Lord, and he will lift you up." - James 4:10 (NIV)

7. We humbly asked Him to remove all our shortcomings.

"If we confess our sins, he is faithful and will forgive us our sins and purify us from all unrighteousness." - 1 John 1:9 (NIV)

8. We made a list of all persons we had harmed and became willing to make amends to them all.

"Do to others as you would have them do to you." - Luke 6:31 (NIV)

9. We made direct amends to such people whenever possible, except when to do so would injure them or others.

"Therefore, if you are offering your gift at the altar and remember that your brother has something against you, leave your gift there in front of the altar. First go and be reconciled to your brother; then come and offer your gift." - Matthew 5:23-24 (NIV)

10. We continue to take personal inventory and when we were wrong, promptly admitted it.

"So, if you think you are standing firm, be careful that you don't fall!" - 1 Corinthians 10:12 (NIV)

11. We sought through prayer and meditation to improve our conscious contact with God, praying only for knowledge of His will for us, and power to carry that out.

"Let the word of Christ dwell in you richly." - Colossians 3:16

(NIV)

12. Having had a spiritual experience as the result of these steps, we try to carry this message to others and practice these principles in all our affairs.

> "Brothers, if someone is caught in a sin, you who are spiritual should restore them gently. But watch yourself, or you also may be tempted." - Galatians 6:1 (NIV)

In addition to the 12 Steps, Celebrate Recovery also follows 8 Recovery Principles that are based on the Beatitudes from the Sermon on the Mount. These principles provide further guidance on how to apply the 12 Steps in daily life and build a strong foundation for lasting change.

8 Recovery Principles and how they relate with Scripture

1. Realize I'm not God; I admit that I am powerless to control my tendency to do the wrong thing and that my life is unmanageable. (Step 1)

   > "You're blessed when you're at the end of your rope. With less of you there is more of God and his rule." - Matthew 5:3 (MSG)

2. Earnestly believe that God exists, that I matter to Him and that He has the power to help me recover. (Step 2)

   > "You're blessed when you feel you've lost what is most dear to you. Only then can you be embraced by the One most dear to you." - Matthew 5:4 (MSG)

3. Consciously choose to commit all my life and will to Christ's care and control. (Step 3)

   > "You're blessed when you're content with just who you are—no more, no less. That's the moment you find yourselves proud owners of everything that can't be bought." - Matthew 5:5 (MSG)

4. Openly examine and confess my faults to myself, to God, and to someone I trust. (Steps 4 and 5)

> "You're blessed when you get your inside world—your mind and heart—put right. Then you can see God in the outside world." - Matthew 5:8 (MSG)

5. Voluntarily submit to any and all changes God wants to make in my life and humbly ask Him to remove my character defects. (Steps 6 and 7)

> "You're blessed when you've worked up a good appetite for God. He's food and drink in the best meal you'll ever eat." - Matthew 5:6 (MSG)

6. Evaluate all my relationships. Offer forgiveness to those who have hurt me and make amends for harm I've done to others when possible, except when to do so would harm them or others. (Steps 8 and 9)

> "You're blessed when you care. At the moment of being 'care-full,' you find yourselves cared for." - Matthew 5:7 (MSG);
>
> "You're blessed when you can show people how to cooperate instead of compete or fight. That's when you discover who you really are, and your place in God's family." Matthew 5:9 (MSG)

7. Reserve a daily time with God for self-examination, Bible reading, and prayer in order to know God and His will for my life and to gain the power to follow His will. (Steps 10 and 11)
8. Yield myself to God to be used to bring this Good News to others, both by my example and my words. (Step 12)

> "You're blessed when your commitment to God provokes persecution. The persecution drives you even deeper into God's kingdom." - Matthew 5:10 (MSG)

If you would like to learn more about Celebrate Recovery or find a local group, you can do so on their direct website at **www.celebraterecovery.com**. If you want a 12-Step addiction group that is not Christian-based, check out Alcoholics Anonymous at **www.aa.org** or Narcotics Anonymous at

www.na.org. And, while this link is for Alcoholics Anonymous, they have listings for online Zoom meetings 24 hours per day so there is support available whenever you need it: **https://aa-intergroup.org/meetings/**.

If outpatient treatment is not enough for you, look into inpatient options. Rehab programs are extremely expensive. A sizable percentage of people who have addictions also have co-existing mental health disorders. Good rehab programs assess for co-existing disorders and trauma to stabilize your mental health and your addiction at the same time. Paid programs offer better services. However, if you are completely broke and need help, SAMHSA can help you locate free rehabs. Keep in mind, these are the same rehabs homeless people go to and the quality of care may not be as high. That said, if you need help, you can find help. You can go to SAMHSA's website at **www.samhsa.gov/find-help** or call them at 800-662-HELP (4357).

And finally, be aware that maintaining sobriety is an ongoing process. While not implying permission to slip, be aware that setbacks happen. People frequently relapse before achieving long-lasting or permanent sobriety. If you do experience a relapse, treat it as a learning experience. Assess what went wrong, what you could have done differently, and seek support to help you get back on track. When you make life changes to get yourself on track as quickly as possible after a relapse, you are retraining your brain to become a sober person.

CHAPTER 14
For parents

Are you a new parent? If so, congratulations! Children are a blessing, a lot of work, and a huge responsibility. This is the most important job you will ever have. You are responsible for their physical, mental, and emotional development. Parenting requires addressing potential inappropriate or harmful behaviors and actively monitoring who could be around your children. Just because someone may seem okay to you does not mean they would be a good influence on your child. You are an adult; children need someone to step in to protect them and that is your job. This involves setting clear boundaries around your work and lifestyle, and also being vigilant regarding monitoring your children's exposure to sexual material, situations, and inappropriate people. It is possible that nobody did this for you, so you may not know how.

Some great books are:
- "Parenting From the Inside Out: How a Deeper Self-Understanding Can Help You Raise Children Who Thrive" by Daniel J. Siegel and Mary Hartzell
- "The Whole-Brained Child: 12 Revolutionary Strategies to Nurture Your Child's Developing Mind" by Daniel J. Siegel and Tina Payne Bryson
- "Safe House: How Emotional Safety Is the Key to Raising Kids Who Live, Love, and Lead Well" by Joshua Straub, PhD
- "Good Pictures Bad Pictures: Porn-Proofing Today's Young Kids" by Kristen A. Jenson

As a former sex worker, you are probably concerned about whether your past occupation has or could impact your relationship with your children. First, it is important to understand that the way children view their parent's involvement in sex work will vary widely based upon their ages, backgrounds, and experiences. A lot will depend upon what your children witnessed, if they were aware of what you were doing, how they found out, and whether or not their own friends know about your past.

Even if you tried to keep what you were doing secret, children can often sense when a parent is doing something secretive or taboo. While young children may not fully understand what sex work entails, adolescents may have a deeper understanding of the risks and consequences involved, and could struggle with feelings of shame, embarrassment, or resentment towards you. Your children's views on your past involvement in sex work could change over time as they grow and mature. Adult children of sex workers often hold a more complex perspective on their parent's involvement in the sex industry since they are more aware of the broader issues involved and have a deeper appreciation for the challenges and risks that their parent faced.

Your occupation does not define who a child is, although it might contribute to the experiences they have while growing up. What you did for work is just a part of who you were, and children grow up with a wide range of experiences and perspectives that go way beyond their parent's occupation. Children have their own challenges, dreams, and goals that they are focused on. As a parent, you cannot protect your children from everything, but you can and should support and validate their experiences and try to understand their unique perspectives.

First, you need to be consciously aware that your children might face stigma or other challenges as a direct result of your past involvement in sex work. This could include bullying from their peers or feeling embarrassment about your occupation.

If your children's friends find out

To highlight an example, let's imagine that a teenage boy's friends discover naked photos, prostitution advertising, or pornography videos of his mother. His reaction will vary depending on his personality, relationship with his mother, and the dynamics of his friendships. Everyone's experience and reactions will be unique. However, some possible reactions could include:

- Embarrassment: The teenager might feel extremely embarrassed or ashamed that his friends have seen his mother in such a vulnerable and private situation.
- Anger: He could become angry at his friends for looking at, sharing, or making inappropriate comments about what they discovered about his mother.
- Frustration: He may feel upset and frustrated regarding the whole situation, especially if he perceives this as an invasion of his mother's privacy.
- Defensiveness: He might feel the need to defend his mother's honor by fighting or confronting his friends over it.
- Anxiety: He could become stressed out over the possibility of her past being further shared, circulated, or lead to reputational harm for his family.
- Isolation: He may feel the need to distance himself from his friends to protect his mother's privacy or his own emotional well-being.
- Need for support: He could need to speak with a counselor or other trusted adult to help him process his feelings and determine how to best manage the situation.

Your child finding out about your sexual past may be one of your worst nightmares. However, it is best that you have this talk voluntarily before it gets forced on your child. Yes, in an ideal world, it might be best to keep it secret forever. But these days with the internet, you cannot assume that anything will stay secret anymore. That is not reality. It can damage your child and further break your trust bond if he discovers your past some other way and is blindsided by it.

When a mother shares her past experiences with her teenager, it creates trust and transparency within their relationship. The son who knows about his mother's past would be less shocked or in disbelief when his friends bring up the topic. Being prepared to address the situation and having confidence to respond happens from him being forewarned. He may still be embarrassed or angry, but it will be much easier for him to maintain control. This open communication fosters a stronger mother-son bond which is crucial if he later faces sensitive discussions with his friends. It allows him to feel emotionally supported which will help him to navigate these conversations while protecting his mother's privacy. And, through the foreknowledge of his mother's experience, he develops the empathy required for mitigating the situation with compassion and maturity.

On the other hand, if the same son were to learn about his mother's past through friends, the initial shock and disbelief will be quite overwhelming. This unexpected revelation can cause confusion, anger, or resentment towards both his mother for not sharing the information and also toward his friends for making it public. In this case, he might even experience anxiety and fear, worrying about the potential impact on his family's reputation and his relationships with friends. As you can see, not knowing in advance can add-on additional unnecessary trauma to the whole situation for children. And, in all reality, it is just a matter of time before they eventually find out.

In conclusion, establishing trust and open communication between you and your children is essential for maintaining strong relationships and dealing with sensitive topics. Have this conversation in an appropriate way based upon the age and maturity level of your children. While surprises can spark challenging situations, having prior knowledge and understanding empowers your kids to navigate those difficult moments confidently and compassionately. A parent openly sharing their past experiences with their children promotes trust and empathy while also teaching their children the importance of taking responsibility for one's actions, especially during times of adversity.

Your child(ren) inappropriately exposed

In an ideal world, your children would not have seen anything inappropriate. However, ideal and reality are often not the same. If you are reading this section, your children were probably exposed in a way they should not have been. If your child has been exposed to inappropriate material or situations as a result of your sex work, it is important to be honest and transparent about what has occurred and address these issues in a sensitive and responsible manner. So, let's deal with that.

Multiple partners. It is not healthy for children to see a revolving door of partners. If that was what your adult children saw, you cannot do anything about it now except have a real discussion about it. If your children are still at home, do not let them see your dates or romantic partners unless it is serious enough that you are moving in together. You may think it is your life and you can do whatever you want, however, children learn by observing and you are teaching them. This can lead to your children growing up with attachment disorders, trust issues, an inability to maintain a stable relationship, low self-esteem, and difficulty with academics. You don't want that future for your kids.

Sexual material. Exposure to sexual material or situations can have a profound impact on a child's emotional and psychological well-being. Ensure anything with nudity—which could even include your cell phone or computer—is not accessible by your children. Studies show it can be traumatic and affect children for years to come when they are exposed to sexual content at early ages. Young children feel overwhelmed, confused, or frightened by what they have heard or seen, and may struggle with feelings of anxiety, guilt, or shame. Avoid minimizing or dismissing their experiences and strive to provide them with age-appropriate information and support. As a parent, it is your job to acknowledge and validate your children's feelings and to offer them support and reassurance as they navigate the resulting complex emotions. Seek separate counseling for both yourself and your child.

Substance abuse. This is two-fold: your children could have seen substance use or they could have been directly exposed to alcohol or drugs. While not healthy for children to see, simply witnessing is significantly better than if they were given something. The reasons people give alcohol and drugs to children ranges from for their own entertainment reasons, to keep the child preoccupied or quiet while the adults do something else, or to exploit the children. People who are under the influence are more likely to make irrational choices as well.

Domestic violence. While research is limited, there is some evidence that shows domestic violence is higher for people within the sex industry. If your children witnessed that, it could affect their own level of safety and confidence. If your children were hurt, they may have long-term psychological wounds.

Sexual abuse. If you still have young children, be aware of who you permit around them. Also, do not allow your children to go unsupervised. Most of the people you know will be fine, however the sex industry is a perverted industry where boundaries are regularly crossed. Those factors combined with a higher rate of substance use can put your children at risk for being inappropriately touched, shown something they should not see, or given substances. Parents within the adult industry need to be even more protective of their children than parents in other lines of work.

If you were not careful enough: apologize, take responsibility for not protecting them, and make sure your children get proper therapy. Depending on who the abuser was, you may not be permitted to talk with your child about it without compromising your case. This is really tough. However, you can still let your children know that you are sorry and want to be there as support in any way they need.

Never minimize what your children tell you they experienced, even if it seems minor from your perspective. If your children view something as a trauma, it most likely is one for them. This is especially important to say because people who have experienced many big-T traumas (severe traumas) feel that others are exaggerating when their trauma seems less severe. People who have been traumatized a lot may not recognize danger or how traumatic something is as quickly because trauma has become normal for them. However, when a child experiences trauma, it is a healthy reaction to freak out or request help, and how you respond will teach them for life whether it is okay for them to defend themselves and seek external support. Please do not mess that up.

Let me be clear, these situations also happen to children in families without sex work. However, the risk is higher for people who have sex professions, deviant lifestyles, and/or do drugs. While I am not accusing anyone of anything, I want to be inclusive of the common things that occur for this population.

All of the above exposures can cause attachment issues for your children, behavioral problems, emotional issues, and trust issues. They may have been neglected. As a worse-case scenario, they might have been given drugs or abused. All of the above scenarios warrant counseling. Your children need you to take responsibility and not minimize. They need loving support and to feel safe speaking with you.

I did not write this section to make you feel bad for traumas that you cannot go back and fix. I wrote this so that you will be aware that, if your children were exposed, they will have issues. If they are still young, you can get them into therapy to start getting help. If they are older, that does not mean they are healed. Years may have passed but, unless they got help, their adult lives are likely still being negatively affected by what they experienced and will continue to be. As a parent, you need to know this and be supportive of your children in the present. Take responsibility for your role. Apologize for anything they witnessed or experienced as children. Offer your nonjudgmental support and do not defend yourself. Help them get into therapy. If this is what you are currently going through, you should also seek therapy for yourself, too.

CHAPTER 15
Trauma

Childhood neglect, sexual abuse, physical abuse, family dysfunction, exposure to violence or other traumatic events all significantly increase the likelihood of engaging in adult industry work later in life. Statistics show sex workers have a substantially higher rate of adverse childhood experiences than other occupations. Of course it is true that not all sex workers have experienced trauma, and not all individuals who have experienced trauma will enter the adult industry.

There is a plethora of diverse and multifaceted reasons for entering sex work. For some, sex work may be a personal choice, while for others, it may be driven by economic necessity or other factors unrelated to trauma. And then there are many who were forced to enter the sex industry, remain working, or intensify their involvement—which also creates trauma. Having a history of trauma heightens vulnerability for homelessness, substance abuse, and mental health issues, all which increase the likelihood of engaging in adult industry work as a means of survival. Additionally, lack of education, poverty, limited opportunities, and other social and economic factors can also contribute to the decision to enter the sex industry.

It is crucial to consider the potential impact of trauma on the mental health and well-being of sex workers. Individuals with a history of trauma may be at a higher risk of experiencing depression, anxiety, post-traumatic stress disorder (PTSD), and other mental health challenges. The nature of sex work, which involves exposure to dangerous situations, stigma, and discrimination, often exacerbates mental health issues. Understanding the nuanced relationship between trauma and sex work is necessary for informed policy and practice, providing appropriate support services, and challenging the stigma and discrimination often faced.

If you have experienced trauma, find a therapist who specializes in trauma. Ideally, you should look for a therapist who understands sex workers as well. Finding such an experienced therapist will require a bit of research, but it will be worth it for the additional support and understanding. Here are some steps to help you find the right therapist:

- <u>Online search</u>: Start by doing a targeted online search using keywords like "therapist," "counselor," "former sex workers," "sex work support," or "sex worker counseling." This will help you find therapists who have experience or a specialization in this area. Since licensing varies between counselors and coaches, you may be able to locate a life coach who specializes in helping sex workers move forward in their lives. A coach won't heal your past trauma like a counselor can but, if you cannot find an appropriate counselor, you can hire a sex worker specialist coach and a therapist for trauma. Coaching and counseling often nicely complement each other since they are related, yet distinct, fields.
- <u>Local organizations</u>: Reach out to local organizations or support groups that work with or advocate for sex workers. They may have a list of recommended therapists or be able to connect you with someone who has relevant experience.
- <u>Professional directories</u>: Use professional directories and databases such as Psychology Today, GoodTherapy, or the National Association of Social Workers to search for therapists who have experience working with former sex workers. Filter your search by expertise, location, and insurance.
- <u>Referrals</u>: Ask other sex workers, friends, family, or healthcare providers for recommendations. They might know of therapists who have experience with this specific population.
- <u>Consultation</u>: When contacting potential therapists, ask about their experience working with former sex

workers. Be open about your needs and inquire about their training, certifications, and approach to therapy.
- Assess the fit: It is essential to find a therapist you feel comfortable with and who understands your unique situation. Schedule an initial appointment to determine if the therapist's style and approach align with your needs and preferences.

Expect finding the right therapist to take time. It is okay to consult with several professionals before making your final choice. The most important thing is to find someone you trust and who can provide the support and understanding you need.

Trauma-specific therapies

Now, back to trauma-specific therapy. There are numerous ways to treat trauma. Talk therapy (also known as counseling and psychotherapy) is the most well-known form of therapy but is not nearly as targeted for helping you heal from trauma as many of the others:

Cognitive Behavioral Therapy (CBT): CBT focuses on identifying and changing maladaptive thought patterns and behaviors that result from traumatic experiences. This approach can help you develop healthier coping strategies and increase your resilience.

Trauma-Focused Cognitive Behavioral Therapy (TF-CBT): TF-CBT is a specific form of CBT designed for trauma. It combines traditional CBT techniques with trauma-specific interventions to help you process traumatic events and develop healthier coping skills.

Eye Movement Desensitization and Reprocessing (EMDR): EMDR is a unique non-drug therapy that uses bilateral stimulation (eye movements, tapping, or auditory tones) to process and integrate traumatic memories, reducing their emotional impact.

Prolonged exposure therapy: This approach involves gradually confronting and processing traumatic memories through revisiting the trauma in a controlled therapeutic environment (imaginal exposure) and facing trauma-related situations in real life (in-vivo exposure).

Group therapy: Group therapy can be an effective treatment by providing a supportive environment to develop coping strategies, learn from others, and share experiences. Group therapy is usually facilitated by a mental health professional or is peer-led. There are even support groups targeted for specific types of traumas.

Psychopharmacology: Medication is often prescribed as an adjunct to therapy when you experience severe symptoms related to trauma: depression, high anxiety, or sleep disturbances. Common medications for trauma-related symptoms include anti-anxiety medications, antidepressants, and sleep aids.

Somatic therapy: These therapies focus on the connection between the mind and the body. They process trauma by releasing physical tension and restoring balance to the nervous system. Examples include somatic experiencing, sensorimotor psychotherapy, and trauma-sensitive yoga.

Expressive arts therapies: Dance, drama, music, and art therapies are an alternative way for you to process and express your trauma—particularly when traditional talk therapy is not appealing or has been ineffective. These therapies facilitate emotional healing by allowing you to express your experiences through creative means.

Mindfulness and meditation: Mindfulness-based practices like deep breathing, progressive muscle relaxation, and meditation increase your emotional regulation skills, reduce anxiety, and develop self-awareness. They can be incorporated into daily life or integrated into other therapeutic approaches.

Self-help and coping strategies: In addition to formal treatment, you can manage your trauma-related symptoms through self-help and coping strategies, good sleep hygiene, regular exercise, maintaining a routine, doing things you enjoy, seeking social support, and nutrition.

Cranial Electrotherapy Stimulation (CES): CES devices are a non-drug treatment which deliver a microcurrent through the brain to stimulate and modulate specific groups of nerve cells. Studies have shown that this is effective for reducing PTSD symptoms, anxiety, depression, and insomnia. The most famous mental health CES device is called Alpha-Stim. It is FDA-approved and requires a prescription.

Since I have lived a traumatic life, I have tried most of the above listed treatments to heal myself. In my case, I found that cleaning up my diet had a profound effect on my mental health and ability to cope. When I ate sugar, my mental health would quickly go downhill. Alcohol is considered a sugar, so for the past many years I have not drank and have also monitored my diet to remain mentally stable. Out of the above listed trauma treatments, the two that made the greatest impact on my PTSD were EMDR and Alpha-Stim CES. Other techniques I found helpful in previous years were psychopharmacology, TF-CBT, and group therapy.

When it came to the chronic anxiety that I could not shake even after I quit the adult industry, I tried everything. For me, everything was a temporary Band-Aid at best and my anxiety persisted. That was until I found Alpha-Stim. In the United States, a prescription is required to purchase an Alpha-Stim device and the machine itself is pricey (almost $1000). There are hundreds of peer-reviewed studies on the effectiveness of CES devices on mental health, even showing that it is more effective than Xanax. It does not instantly calm you the way Xanax does. Alpha-Stim is not a drug to temporarily make you feel better; CES is low-volt electricity that realigns your brain to fix what causes the anxiety in the first place. My own experience was that I used it an hour each day for 60 consecutive days and it cured my anxiety. Yes, I said it *cured* me. It was quite literally the best money I have ever spent in my life. If you have anxiety, you should research Alpha-Stim, speak with your psychiatrist, and ask if this option could be correct for you.

Since I mentioned EMDR, and personally felt it was the most helpful PTSD treatment for me, I will explain it more so you can decide if it is a treatment you want to pursue for yourself. Eye Movement Desensitization and Reprocessing (EMDR) is a non-drug evidence-based psychotherapy technique developed in the late 1980s by Dr. Francine Shapiro that is often effective in reducing post-traumatic stress disorder (PTSD). EMDR is based on the Adaptive Information Processing (AIP) theory with the point of view that the human brain can naturally process and integrate traumatic experiences. When that processing system gets blocked, the traumatic memories are stored in a dysfunctional manner causing psychological distress.

EMDR may be able to help you to process and integrate your distressing memories and recover from the emotional impact of trauma. EMDR therapy is comprised of an eight-phase approach:

1) <u>History and treatment-planning</u>: Your EMDR therapist will gather information about your history, identify the memories to be targeted with EMDR processing, and establish a treatment plan.
2) <u>Preparation</u>: Your therapist will develop self-soothing techniques and coping strategies for you to use during and after your EMDR sessions.
3) <u>Assessment</u>: Your therapist will identify specific thoughts, images, bodily sensations, and emotions from the memory being targeted.
4) <u>Desensitization</u>: Your therapist will guide you through

bilateral stimulation (e.g., tapping or auditory tones) or sets of eye movements while you are focusing on the specific target memory. Through this process, your brain can reprocess the memory correctly which reduces its traumatic emotional impact.
5) <u>Installation</u>: Your therapist will then reprogram your negative beliefs related to the target memory and work with you to strengthen positive beliefs.
6) <u>Body scan</u>: You will conduct a full mental scan of your body to determine whether you still feel any residual physical sensations within your body related to the traumatic memory. If you do, you will continue processing until the physical sensations are no longer triggered.
7) <u>Closure</u>: In closing the session, your therapist will help you return to a state of emotional equilibrium. Afterward, the two of you will review the previously discussed self-soothing techniques for you to use between sessions.
8) <u>Reevaluation</u>: At your next session, the therapist will do a check-in to evaluate your progress and adjust your treatment plan as needed.

Eye Movement Desensitization and Reprocessing (EMDR) facilitates the reprocessing and integration of traumatic memories which helps you to heal from trauma-related disorders, PTSD, panic, anxiety, and depression. EMDR works extremely quickly, sometimes in as little as a single session, and can be life changing. It is crucial that you find someone who is well-trained to ensure that the therapy is conducted safely and effectively.

EMDR is an independent skill. This means practitioners can be bad at other therapies yet good at EMDR or they can be great therapists yet bad at EMDR. The safest way to choose an experienced and qualified EMDR therapist is by going to **https://www.emdria.org/find-an-emdr-therapist**, entering your zip code, and then further filter your list by clicking the "Only Show EMDR Certified Therapists" box within the left navigational bar.

Emdria is considered the gold standard of EMDR training and certification.

When it comes to you, your most effective treatment for trauma may vary depending on your unique needs, preferences, and the nature of your traumatic experience(s). It can take working with a trauma-focused mental health professional plus trial and error to find the most effective treatment approach that works for you.

CHAPTER 16
Sexual after-effects

Working in the sex industry usually leads to experimentation. Chances are you are familiar with most of these. Maybe you did these things for work, maybe they are activities you enjoy in your personal life. I am including them here because they are significantly less common in the mainstream world.

BDSM

Lots of people in the adult industry are into aspects of BDSM. BDSM stands for Bondage, Discipline, Sadism, and Masochism. BDSM is all about exploring different sensations, emotions, and power exchanges in a safe and controlled environment. It is a fascinating and diverse world which includes many types of consensual practices: role-play, power dynamics, impact play, sensory deprivation, and bondage. The key to a positive BDSM experience is trust, consent, and clear communication.

B = Bondage. Bondage is physically restraining someone using rope, handcuffs, zip ties, scarves, or other types of devices. Being deprived of movement in a semi-permanent way (as opposed to just being held down) makes someone extremely vulnerable. Helplessness can create a sense of anticipation, excitement, or fear which heightens the experience for some people.

D = Discipline. Discipline is like parenting. One person makes the rules and there are consequences or punishments if those rules are broken. The person in charge is referred to as the Dominant or Top, and the submissive person is called a Sub or bottom. Discipline can create a sense of structure and control that leads to pleasure.

S = Sadism. A sadist enjoys inflicting pain, humiliating people, causing discomfort and derives sexual pleasure from doing so. Within the context of BDSM, sadism is a consensual activity.

M = Masochism. Masochism refers to deriving pleasure from pain, being humiliated, or the feeling of discomfort, within the bounds of consent. Masochists enjoy these sensations. Like sadism, masochism should always be consensual. Generally, it does not involve serious harm.

BDSM can also involve a variety of other practices and fetishes: role-playing, dominance and submission (D/s), sensation play, impact play, and cuckoldry, to name a few. Positive and enjoyable BDSM experiences establish consent, boundaries, and clear communication within a safe, trusting environment.

If these are sexual practices that you absolutely must keep in your life, Fetlife.com is the social network/dating site for finding likeminded fetish sexual partners. The profiles are extremely detailed. You can post exactly what you are into and what you are looking for, and people can find you based on that criterion. Within the context of open communication, consent, and respect, BDSM can remain a fulfilling and enjoyable part of your personal and private life.

Littles / Middles

Now I will explain the fascinating world of littles and middles. These terms may be new to some. They refer to unique identities within the realm of age play and the BDSM community. Age play is a form of role-playing where you assume a younger age role, often to explore various aspects of your personality or fulfill fantasies. Littles and middles are individuals who express themselves though adapting a much younger persona.

Littles take on the role or identify of a young child aging from birth up to 11-years-old. Sometimes this manifests as playing with toys, coloring, or watching cartoons. Middles, on the other hand, typify the role of pre-teens or teenagers, usually between the ages of 12 and 17 and often enjoy attending social events with other middles, playing video games, listening to music, or doing other activities normal for that age range.

Being a little or middle is not about sexualizing minors. No. Instead, it is a consensual adult activity that allows you to tap into distinct younger aspects of yourself in a safe and controlled environment. For both littles and middles, this type of play provides a safe space to explore their desires, create experiences, and feel emotions. Age play involves a caregiver whose responsibility is to nurture and protect the little or middle, and that caretaking creates a trusting and affectionate bond.

The reasons why someone becomes a little can vary greatly. For some, engaging in age play as a little might be related to past trauma, while for others, it could simply be a form of self-expression, enjoyment, or exploration. In cases of early trauma, you may be drawn to age play as a way to revisit, process, or heal from past experiences. By assuming the role of a little, you might feel a sense of safety, comfort, and control that was lacking during the original traumatic event. Age play has the potential to be therapeutic, allowing you to rewrite your narrative in a consensual and safe environment. Not all littles or middles became so due to past trauma. Many littles engage in age play for reasons unrelated to their childhood experiences. Age play allows you to be more creative, happy, or at ease by adopting a younger persona and taking part in activities associated with that age.

This is another category I have personal experience with.

In my case, my being a little was related to early life traumas. I won't detail what my traumas were, but I do feel that it is important to say the ages I identified as. Emotionally, I did not grow up gradually; I jumped almost a decade each time. I am sharing my story so those who identify in a similar type of way will know they are not alone.

Until I was in my late thirties, I identified as a 4-year-old. This was not a fetish for me; I knew I was an adult, but I also knew I was emotionally stuck as a child. I had the innocence, curiosity, and constant wonder of a small child. And that was the me who entered the adult industry. Given my overly trusting nature, it is surprising that it took so long for a pimp to manipulate me. I told him very early on that I was a little. In response, he took exceptionally good care of me and made me feel loved and safe, something I lacked when I was actually 4 years old. And due to my naivety, I could not bring myself to believe that he was exploiting me until it had continued for an extended period. This was because, for the first time in my life, I felt safe, loved, and accepted. So, even after I realized what was happening, I allowed it to continue because I did not know how to cope without him. Had our relationship not had that toxic element, I believe his presence and caring love could have healed me.

Then I had a relationship with a Daddy Dom who was a physical and emotional sadist. He understood my little, and I was willing to do anything for him. He was not a pimp, which was great. He loved "take down" play and would regularly chase me down to rape me. I was accustomed to men being rough, so this did not seem unreasonable to me. Most of the time, he took good care of my young little...until his emotional sadistic side needed to torture me. Even though I was a willing participant, I was repeatedly and severely traumatized. When a friend helped me to leave him, I grew into a middle.

I was a 15-year-old middle for a few years. The best way I can explain being a middle: it is like reliving the teenage years, with all the same teenage desires, interests, and some recklessness (although less because I had the knowledge of an older woman). I even dated a much younger man because I felt we were on par. A trauma caused me to grow out of the middle stage.

Overnight, I became an emotional 22-year-old. The majority of my friends at that time were half my chronological age. I could identify with 18 to 25-year-olds and, since I looked significantly younger than I was, it did not seem weird to them to hang out with me. They liked me too; I fit in. However, severe trauma forced me to grow up practically overnight again from 22 to my mid-thirties.

In real life, I am now 50 years old. That is weird. I think mentally I am still in my mid-thirties, and I like this age. I am self-sufficient, I have developed boundaries, I am a great mother. For me, being a little and then a middle was not roleplay; it was my life. Some call it lifestyle, but that implies choice and I never felt like this was my choice. This has been my genuine experience.

There is not enough information online about littles and middles, and most of the information is on fetish sites. While researching, I found an online message board for those who truly identify in this way, do not want to grow up, and want to feel understood. It is: **www.ddlgforum.com**.

If you do identify as a little or a middle, I hope you recognize how much easier it can be for someone to manipulate or take advantage of you. Children are easy to manipulate. I was a child in a grown woman sexy body. Are you a child? If so, how can you protect yourself? It is important to think that through. Maybe create a written list of warning signs or assign a trusted mature friend to veto your new friends or relationship partners.

Sex addiction

Addiction is a preoccupation with and loss of control over any behavior or substance despite adverse consequences. Sex addiction is characterized by a persistent and escalating pattern of sexual thoughts, fantasies, or behaviors that interfere with one's daily life, relationships, and emotional well-being. Also called hypersexual disorder, sex addiction is a compulsion to engage in sexual activities and it can change the brain chemistry of the addicted. Like other addictions, it stems from a complex interplay of biological, psychological, and social factors, including your upbringing, brain chemistry, cultural influences, and genetics. Childhood trauma is very highly correlated with addiction in general and even higher for sexual addiction.

Patrick Carnes, the pioneer in sex addiction research, found that 97% of sex addicts had experienced emotional abuse, 74% were physically abused, and 81% were sexually abused. I am going to go into a lot more detail here because often we have assumptions of what constitutes abuse, and abuse includes a lot more than just that. I am writing this in the context of child abuse, but these things also happen to adults by non-parents.

Invasive emotional abuse happens when you are told that you are bad. "Mind rape" is a type of invasive emotional abuse that occurs when your parent makes you feel that your own feelings are not valid and that you should feel another way. Maybe that parent had good intentions, yet you internalized your feelings as being bad or unacceptable which resulted in you learning to numb your feelings in life.

Abandonment is emotional abuse on the opposite end of the spectrum. Your parents were present but emotionally cold with you, refused to share, and did not really listen to you. You justifiably felt like you did not have any love or support. It could have been intentional on their part, or it could have been accidental if they were too busy focusing on their own perceived greater priorities. Emotional abuse injures self-esteem and parent abandonment leads to an unfillable void that can lead to addiction in an attempt to make up a feeling of wholeness.

Physical abuse is violence. You might have been the recipient of the abuse, although early witnessing of physical abuse can also be damaging (such as growing up in a domestic violence household).

Physical abandonment is when your physical needs go unmet. Self-care must be taught. Physical abandonment also includes when there is nobody present to take care of you and you are left by yourself as a child.

Sexual abuse can be invasive, such as in someone directly touching your genitals, subtle invasive by forced hugging or lap sitting, or through comments about your body, development, or romantic feelings that you may have.

Abandonment sexual abuse is the opposite of invasive sexual abuse, and it is the total absence of discussions about hormonal and body changes, sex, or physical pleasure and relationships. If you were sexually abused through abandonment, you may have grown up feeling ashamed of your desire or worried that it meant you had done something wrong. Then, while growing up, you seldom received help because you felt like you could not discuss it with anyone. Early exposure to pornography and early sexual experiences are two more factors that increase sex addiction.

Spiritual abuse is when a parent uses the fear of God to control your actions. Instead of being taught that God is a loving God, you are taught that God will punish you.

Invasive sexual spiritual abuse is when you are taught that sex is dirty and bad instead of attributing sex to be a wonderful marital gift. Fearing sexual repercussions can fuel sex addiction in two ways: (1) it prevents disclosure, and (2) it entices due to the danger of excitement of forbidden fruit pleasures. Anything that can be used to self-medicate and squash feelings can be addictive, and this is especially true for sex. Many sex addicts only find pleasure in forbidden encounters.

Abandonment sexual spiritual abuse directly lacked the healthy modeling you needed while growing up and trust was destroyed by hypocrisy.

Take a minute if you need it. Sometimes people do not realize that they were abused. It can be a hard blow if this is when you are first realizing it. It can also be a relief because now you might understand why you have had difficulty in life, self-medicated, or had other issues. I am going to continue on now with how sex workers are at higher risk for sex addiction.

The sex industry is a unique environment where workers are frequently exposed to various forms of sexual activity and often in excess. The repeated exposure nature of the sex industry can lead to desensitization of sexual stimuli. Since sexual activities are part of the job, over time you might require increasingly intense or varied experiences to achieve the same level of arousal or satisfaction. Desensitization with corresponding higher tolerances contribute to the development of sex addiction.

To cope with the occupational demands, you might have emotionally detached yourself from your clients. If this detachment extended to your personal life, it could lead to difficulties in forming and maintaining healthy, intimate relationships. Many former sex workers have experienced various forms of trauma, including sexual abuse, physical violence, and emotional manipulation. These experiences can cause depression, anxiety, and post-traumatic stress disorder (PTSD), which also increase the risk of developing addictive behaviors, including sex addiction.

Sex addiction can manifest as excessive pornography watching, regularly filming yourself when doing so is not your occupation, compulsive masturbation, engaging in high-risk sexual behaviors, or maintaining multiple affairs. Over time, these behaviors often lead to physical and mental health issues, loss of relationships, and significant consequences like the loss of relationships and financial instability.

In today's fast-paced, interconnected world, sex addiction has become a growing concern for tons of people. You are not alone. Since the invention of smart phones and the subsequent launch of PornHub, pornography viewing and sexual addiction have literally become an epidemic. If you identify as having this problem and want to change, there are ways.

The first step with any addiction, including sexual addiction, is to acknowledge that you have a problem. It takes courage to accept that you have an issue and determination to do so head-on. Embrace your vulnerability and be prepared to put in the necessary work to address your addiction. One of the most critical aspects of recovery is building a strong support network. Confess your struggles with at least one trusted friend, family member, or to a support group. This openness will help you feel less isolated, will give you a sense of accountability, and might provide encouragement during your recovery process.

It is essential to seek professional help. There are coaches, counselors, and psychologists who specialize in sexual addiction. Someone with this specialization can help you identify the root causes of your addiction and work with you to develop a personalized treatment plan. Together you will identify the factors that precede your behavior, your triggers, and come up with alternate behaviors. If you believe you can do this on your own, consciously decide first how many relapses you consider acceptable. And if that many times occur, immediately schedule an appointment for professional help.

During your recovery, setting rigid boundaries is essential. Decide which behaviors are ok and which are not and do not cheat. Many people with sex addiction decide to go cold turkey for pornography and all sexual contact, including masturbation, for a minimum of 90 days to start. When people are not married, they often extend that time. If you have a partner, you need to honestly discuss your problem and explain that you must avoid situations which trigger your addictive behaviors.

Make sure you take care of yourself. Exercise and sports are good stress-relievers and can help you during withdrawals because they are also a physical activity. Eating nutritiously will also make it easier to cope. Adopt a new hobby or volunteer to fill up your time. Journal your emotions. Define your boundaries. What and where needs to be avoided? Will you have to take new routes to avoid passing a specific place? Are there people you need to stop speaking with? Can you be trusted on the computer? Be honest and set boundaries. Celebrate your progress, even if it is slow, and be kind to yourself when setbacks occur. Recovery from sex addiction is a process that takes time and effort, more time than most people expect, and slips may happen. Find an external accountability partner.

In your journey towards healing, you might also consider attending free 12-step programs, such as Sexaholics Anonymous (SA, **www.sa.org**), Sex Addicts Anonymous (SAA, **https://saa-recovery.org/**) or Sex and Love Addicts Anonymous (SLAA, **https://slaafws.org/**). These groups provide a supportive environment and can be a huge help in your recovery process as you realize you are not alone. By attending these groups, you meet people who understand what you are going through and who can suggest ways of coping that are new to you.

Sex addiction affects all levels of society. However, former sex workers are at a heightened risk due to the unique differences within the sex industry professions. Recognizing your vulnerabilities and receiving appropriate support and resources can help you overcome your addiction, build healthier relationships, and lead a happier, more fulfilling life.

If you feel that this is a problem you might have, here are some resources to help:
- "Don't Call it Love" by Patrick Carnes
- "Healing The Wounds of Sexual Addiction" by Mark Laaser
- "Soul Virgins: Redefining Single Sexuality" by Doug Rosenau and Michael Todd Wilson
- Accountable – online accountability app

Sex as self-injury

Sex as Self-Injury (SASI) is a complex and often misunderstood behavior that involves using sexual activity as a means of self-harm. While the topic of self-injury has gained attention in recent years, the study and understanding of SASI remains limited. Sex as self-injury (SASI) is not widely talked about. Just like a cutter makes physical incisions in skin to release pain, emotionally or physically painful sex can be used in a similar way. This is different from sex addiction.

SASI refers to engaging in sexual behavior with the intention of causing physical or emotional harm to oneself. It is a form of self-injury, similar to other self-harming behaviors like cutting, hitting oneself, and burning. The difference between SASI and more traditional forms of self-injury lies in the use of sexual activities as a tool for self-punishment or self-destruction. It does not leave physical marks and so it is more easily adopted by people who feel the need to self-mutilate but cannot afford the marks. This is especially attractive to sex workers.

While I have known many women in the industry who utilized SASI as their method of self-harm, thus far there has been little scientific research into self-harming through sex. This is a new field that needs to be researched within the Western hemisphere since the current studies are from Europe. The reasons people engage in SASI are varied and deeply personal. However, a few common factors have been identified that directly contributing to this behavior:

- Trauma: If you have a history of sexual child abuse, sex trafficking, or another sexual traumatic experience which created a negative mental association with sex, this can lead to later using sex as a form of self-punishment.
- Low self-esteem: Low self-esteem could cause you to use SASI as a means of punishing yourself for perceived flaws or failures.
- Emotional regulation: Like other forms of self-injury, SASI can serve as a coping mechanism if you have difficulty managing overwhelming emotions or are unable to express your feelings in other ways.

The consequences of SASI will likely hurt you socially, physically, and emotionally. Socially it can hurt your public reputation and how people view you. When using sex as self-punishment, you are more likely to engage in dangerous sexual behaviors which increases your risk for sexually transmitted infections (STIs), unintended pregnancies, or even being physically hurt by the other person in a non-sexual way. Since the sex is designed to be punishment, your sex partners are probably people that you do not want to have sex with, including strangers. This can further damage your self-esteem, exacerbate any preexisting mental health issues, and strain your personal relationships. By cheapening yourself and having free sex with anyone who wants to touch you, you get that very painful reinforcement of being unworthy. If you were a previously pimped sex worker, you might participate in SASI as a method of punishing yourself for your past.

SASI is not sex addiction

While Sex as Self-Injury (SASI) and sex addiction both share some similarities in terms of engaging in sexual behaviors, they are distinct concepts with different underlying motivations and psychological processes. Understanding these differences is crucial in securing appropriate support and treatment for either of these conditions.

Motivation: The primary difference between SASI and sex addiction is the motivation behind the behaviors. In SASI, you engage in sexual activities with the intention of causing physical or emotional harm to yourself as a form of self-punishment or self-destruction. In contrast, sex addiction is characterized by your compulsive need to engage in sexual activities to experience pleasure, cope with stress, or escape from negative emotions.

Self-injury vs. compulsion: SASI is a form of self-injury where you use sex as a means to inflict harm on yourself. This is different from sex addiction which is considered a behavioral addiction and driven by an uncontrollable urge or compulsion to engage in sexual activities.

Emotional outcomes: Another distinction between SASI and sex addiction is the emotional outcome of the behavior. In SASI, you experience feelings of guilt, shame, or self-loathing both during and after the punishing sexual activities. There is no positive relief, the entire experience is negative. Whereas in sex addiction, you do feel temporary relief and pleasure during the sexual act, which is only later followed by guilt, shame, or regret based on how your compulsive behavior negatively impacts your life.

Treatment approaches: Given the differences in motivation and psychological processes between SASI and sex addiction, the treatment approaches for these conditions are also distinct. For SASI, therapeutic interventions often focus on addressing the underlying issues contributing to your self-injurious behavior by utilizing EMDR to heal the sexual trauma you experienced and DBT to teach you self-love and provide a sense of worth. In contrast, treatment for sex addiction involves addressing the compulsive nature of the behavior and uses similar approaches to those employed in treating other behavioral addictions, gambling addiction, or substance use disorders. Sex addiction treatment usually includes 12-Step programs, individual and group counseling, relapse prevention, and sometimes even inpatient rehabilitation.

As you can see, while SASI and sex addiction both involve sexual behaviors, they are distinct conditions with different underlying motivations, emotional outcomes, and treatment approaches. Few people have heard of SASI so it can be falsely associated with sex addiction. Recognizing the differences between them and knowing which one applies to you is essential for receiving appropriate support and therapeutic intervention.

People think that when they leave the sex industry, they will be done. Unfortunately, it is not quite so simple. Sexual after-effects are common. The sex industry is taboo in itself, and it draws even more taboo. You may be happy with your sexual self, and you may have no problem finding a partner in the normal world, or you might realize that you have sexual differences that are not considered normal. I purposely chose not to include polyamory or swinging in this chapter (even though they are also common) because I view them more as personal lifestyle choices instead of aftereffects.

CHAPTER 17
Core beliefs

Differing religious values

Beliefs and values are deeply personal and there are many different religions, so it is essential to find your correct path as you navigate your new life. This may involve exploring various religions or perspectives to determine which, if any, makes the most sense to you and will support your healing. To find the one that resonates with you, evaluate their core beliefs and practices. You can explore further by reading their texts, talking to people who practice these faiths, or visiting places of worship. Remember, there's no rush – finding your spiritual path is a personal journey, and you should take whatever time you need to find what makes sense to you. I will list a few below to give you a starting point.

Christianity: If you like idea of a loving and personal relationship with God, Christianity may be the correct fit. Most Christian religions believe in a single God who exists as the Holy Trinity: Father, Son (Jesus Christ), and Holy Spirit, and believe that Jesus was the human representation as the Son of God. Jesus Christ's teachings provide a moral compass with his life, death, and resurrection pathing the way for our salvation. Worship, prayer, fellowship, tithes, baptism, and reading the Bible are important aspects for Christianity. The different denominations interpret the Bible differently and vary in their rituals and beliefs, so if the New Testament of the Bible and Jesus resonates as truth for you, search for a denomination that most aligns with your core beliefs.

Judaism: Jesus was a Jew. Christians believe that Jesus was

the Messiah and that is why Christianity began. In direct contrast, Judaism does not recognize Jesus as the savior, nor do they recognize the New Testament at all. The Torrah is Judaism's holy book and it is comprised from the first 5 books of the Old Testament in the Bible. Judaism traces its roots back to Abraham and the covenant he made with God. Key beliefs include the concept of one God, the importance of following God's commandments, and the idea of a future Messiah who will come to redeem the Jewish people. Major branches of Judaism include Orthodox, Conservative, and Reform, each with its unique interpretations and practices.

Islam: Like both Judaism and Christianity, Islam also believes in one God (Allah). Although Islam recognizes Jesus as a prophet, they do not believe he was the savior and instead believe that Muhammad was the final prophet. Islam's holy book, the Quran, includes some of the books of the Bible plus additional text, is considered the word of God, and provides all guidance for every aspect of life. Islam is much more structured and disciplined than Christianity with daily prayer being performed five times each day and mandatory fasting during the month of Ramadan for added self-discipline, worship, and spiritual reflection. The Five Pillars of Islam provide an intense sense of unity among Muslims.

Hinduism: Hinduism has a strong focus on reincarnation, dharma, karma, and the pursuit of spiritual liberation. Hinduism also recognizes multiple gods and goddesses, yet also acknowledges a single Supreme Being or "Brahman." This is an Indian-based religion but there are people who practice Hinduism all over the world.

Buddhism: If you do not believe in any god yet seek a spiritual path focused on personal growth, inner peace, and compassion for all beings, Buddhism could be a great fit. Through meditation and mindful living, you work towards enlightenment (also called nirvana) and learn to overcome suffering. Buddhism's Four Noble Truths and the Eightfold Path provide a framework for achieving enlightenment and overcoming suffering.

Paganism: Paganism is a collection of spiritual practices, beliefs, and paths which emphasize a deep connection to nature, natural cycles, and a reverence for multiple gods and goddesses. Their rituals and ceremonies often mark celestial events, important life milestones, or seasonal changes. Paganism is often expressed through meditation, energy work, offerings to deities, magic, or the manipulation of natural energies to achieve desired outcomes. There is no central authority or rigid dogma in Paganism, which allows for a broad range of interpretations and approaches.

Religious viewpoints vary when it comes to sex work. There are basic religious generalities based on historical, cultural contexts, and dogma perspective. Like most things, it is important to not make assumptions or assume that everyone in any group will immediately disapprove of you for your past.

Since moral judgments often originate through upbringing or religious values, I want to briefly cover how the various religions' role can influence their members' opinion of sex work. A vast majority of the religions around the world value empathy, understanding, and compassion. Locating these valued traits within someone will allow you to speak with them about your experiences at a level where they hear you instead of judging or discounting you.

The major religions of Christianity, Judaism, and Islam all believe that sex should take place within marriage and are opposed to prostitution. That said, all three also have a strong emphasis on mercy and compassion. Both Christianity and Judaism teach forgiveness, compassion, and understanding, so some may not judge nor condemn those who have a sex work past. Muslims believe in helping and supporting individuals who have faced difficulties in life, including those who participated in the sex industry.

Buddhists consider sex a distraction on the path to enlightenment, so they do not support prostitution. However, Buddhists are not judgmental toward sex workers, either. To my surprise, Hinduism and Paganism have used sex work within their temples. In ancient Near Eastern religions, sacred prostitution was practiced and "qadishtus" were temple sex workers considered to have a divine role. Even today, there are still many places in Asia where sex and prostitution have religious or spiritual significance.

Once you know what you believe, you need to figure out how you feel that you and your past fit into the story. Your own religious beliefs can help you find comfort and support, or they can potentially hinder your healing as you transition out of the sex industry. Do you believe that you are equal to others? Do you feel that you are somehow "less than" due to your past life or occupation? Do you believe you have done anything that is unforgiveable?

If you find that your own views are holding your back, examine why and investigate further to see if what you believe is consistent with the teachings. This is imperative because— even when we feel on par with other people—if we feel inadequate in our God's eyes, we can block ourselves from moving forward and healing. If you are experiencing this, it must be addressed. Spiritual healing assistance after quitting sex work is not easy to find. While many religious organizations offer counseling, support groups, or other resources that can build self-compassion and growth, few address the specific concerns of retired sex workers.

In my case I did not feel worthy of God after leaving the sex industry. I would pray, express how grateful I was and say thank you repeatedly, but I would never ask for anything because I felt that I had no right to ask. At least with Christianity, this was a ridiculous viewpoint and faulty thinking on my part because Jesus did not die only for the good people—his death was specially to save those of us who needed it most. Yes, there was no doubt I had sinned according to my belief system, but I also confessed, repented, and have been reborn since then.

I believed I was broken beyond repair. My pimp would tell me that I could never find anyone to love me, and I had believed him. I was socially awkward and an extreme introvert. Even though I would go to church, I felt like an imposter. This is where a Christian life coach would have been helpful.

Thankfully, I lived abroad at that time in a county where exorcisms were not considered crazy nor abnormal. Going through an exorcism was not my idea, and I did not know beforehand that was their plan. However, being someone who did not believe exorcisms were real before that day, I was in awe of what I experienced. There were definitely spirits cast out of me that day. The next morning, my beautiful red pet fish turned white and disintegrated. I truly belief that—just like the Bible exorcism story with the pigs—the spirits left me and went into the fish. You do not have to believe me; I am just sharing my experience. That exorcism set me free emotionally and spiritually and has allowed me to live my life as a new person with happiness and stability ever since. It is a pity that exorcisms are not more widely available for those who feel they would benefit.

Spirituality & Personal Values: Rediscovering Your Core Beliefs

Spirituality is a deeply personal and subjective connection experience to something greater than oneself. As you previously read, spirituality can be religion, connecting to God, being at one with the Earth Mother, finding a deep sense of purpose, or having a profound understanding of the interconnectedness of all living beings. In all cases, it provides a powerful source of inner resilience during challenging times. Your personal values are the guiding principles and moral compass that shape your decisions, actions, and beliefs. They are often born from your family of origin, your past individual experiences, your culture, or from your religion. When you are in touch with your core values, you are equipped to navigate life's challenges and make decisions that align with your authentic self.

After leaving the sex industry, sometimes it is difficult to know what your core values are. If you were pimped, that can be even more difficult. After an extended time of being told what is important and how to think, you may have to start from scratch to figure it out for yourself. Question your beliefs to see if they really originate from you. I know that sounds ridiculous so I will give you an example. I would regularly hear *"It's better to look good than to feel good."* Isn't that crazy? Yet, I heard it so much that I adopted it as a belief and would later repeat that same sentence to others. But this was not one of my core beliefs and never had been. This is an example of brainwashing that I accepted, incorporated into who I thought I was, and then propagated. Almost a decade later, I realized I was still continuing a false programmed belief, so I let it go. It is tough realizing all the ways we may have been changed that do not align with who we really are or who we want to be, but it is a necessary step for moving forward. Feeling good *is* more important than looking good.

That was just a simple example, and I could give numerous others. Ask yourself, who should pay for dates? How soon should sex occur with a new partner? Is it okay to lie and, if so, under what circumstances? Should all intimate relationships be monogamous? How much alcohol consumption is considered normal in the real world? Is divorce okay? Should both parents work, or should one stay home with the children? Is it okay to have debt? How do you feel about forgiveness? Is violence ever acceptable? This is a list of values that you probably have opinions on, and those opinions may or may not have been distorted by the industry or third parties. Think about them and whether your current behaviors and answers are aligned with your believe system. If you discover contradictions, write them down, pay attention.

The process of introspection identifies your core beliefs that truly matter, paving the way for a more authentic and fulfilling life. Recognizing which beliefs may have been influenced by the sex industry or other external factors is crucial when trying to discover your own core values. As you identify your misaligned beliefs, you can begin to challenge and replace them with values that better align with your true self.

Identifying Misaligned Beliefs

Your beliefs are the lens which you see the world through. Your overall life experiences, actions, and thoughts are all shaped by your individual beliefs. Ideally, your beliefs should align with your core values, thoughts, and actions to create a life that you are proud of. However, sometimes you may believe a false reality or have ideas that conflict with your authentic self. Those are called misaligned beliefs and they hinder your growth and ability to heal. Therefore, it is crucial to identify faulty thinking and misaligned beliefs and replace them with new empowering beliefs.

<u>Understanding Misaligned Beliefs</u>

You would think it would be easy to spot misaligned beliefs since they are thoughts that contradict your core values, authentic self, or long-term goals. Yet these beliefs are often born in external influences, societal norms, family expectations, peer pressure, or past experiences. Often, you may not notice them there. Then, these misaligned beliefs manifest themselves as negative or limiting thought patterns that result in discontentment, unhappiness, or stagnation in your life.

How people get misaligned beliefs:
- Society and culture: Where and with whom we grow up with influences the beliefs we adopt. There

is a constant borage of expectations: relationships, beauty standards, success, gender roles. Sometimes you can subconsciously accept these expectations even though they do not align with your authentic self.
- Childhood upbringing: Your family's traditions, communication styles, and parental values help form your beliefs. Your family-influenced beliefs may hinder your personal growth.
- Past experience and trauma: Experiencing trauma can limit your beliefs about the world. An earlier failed attempt can also impact your beliefs. You may self-sabotage thinking you are not as capable as you are.
- Peer pressure: A desire to be accepted by others may lead you to adopt beliefs that do not align with your authentic self. Doing so disconnects you from your core values and prevents you from living an authentic life.

Identifying and Challenging Misaligned Beliefs

The first step in addressing misaligned beliefs is to become aware of them. You will need to cultivate self-awareness and engage in introspection to identify the beliefs that are holding you back. You can do this through:
- Writing about your thoughts, feelings, and experiences in a journal to uncover underlying beliefs that might be influencing your behaviors and emotions.
- Meditation and mindfulness both increase self-awareness and help you to see any limiting beliefs thought patterns that are not serving you.
- Professional life coaches and counselors can help you identify and address misaligned beliefs while also providing tools for you to improve and grow.

Once you identify misaligned beliefs, challenge them and replace them with more empowering beliefs. This involves questioning the validity of your current beliefs, seeking alternative perspectives, and mentally testing them to see which best aligns with you in a positive way.

A splendid example of this is instead of saying *"I can't ___"* about anything, change that statement to *"I haven't ___ yet."* It is a small switch, yet powerful.

<u>Core beliefs for a healthy you</u>
1) In order to fully embrace your spirituality and personal values, it is essential to cultivate and practice self-compassion. This means treating yourself with the same empathy, understanding, and kindness that you would extend to a good friend. It also means not judging yourself, shaming yourself, or feeling guilty for things you cannot change.
2) Forgiveness is for you, not for the other person. It does not mean that the act did not happen or was forgotten. It means you are now at peace and can move on without it hurting you anymore. You forgive to release your own toxic emotions.
3) Be grateful. By focusing on the positive aspects of life and expressing appreciation for the opportunities to grow and change, you live a happier life in the present with an optimistic outlook and resilience toward future challenges.
4) Supportive and understanding friends, family, and therapists are necessary guides along your self-discovery and personal growth journey. Lean on them for support.
5) You need to periodically evaluate friendships and establish healthy boundaries to honor and protect that which is important to you.
6) Be open to new experiences and perspectives.

The process of self-discovery and personal growth is ongoing and will require continuous effort and commitment. Self-reflect, cultivate self-compassion, and embrace personal growth to find a renewed sense of purpose and self-worth. You deserve it!

CHAPTER 18
Conclusion

This book covered building self-worth after leaving the sex industry, emotional healing, career and education opportunities, physical and mental health, personal finance and budgeting, spirituality and personal values. You also learned the importance of finding a support system, creating balance in life, advocating for change, maintaining progress over the long-term through therapy, and how to protect your legal rights.

This chapter is just a brief summary of the book. Obviously, there will not be many details here. Yet it is a good review after you have read the book and can help you know what you might need to reread later.

The journey to discovering your worth after leaving the sex industry may be long and difficult, but it is worth it. Chapter 1 gave an overview of the different aspects of what this journey looks like to help you move forward with your life. From overcoming stigma to cultivating self-compassion, hopefully you now understand the importance of taking a comprehensive approach to healing and growth.

In chapter 2, we discussed childhood attachment styles. Who you became, your vulnerabilities, and your coping styles were mostly determined while you were still a small child. Knowing this should allow you to have self-compassion as you move forward in life. Your attachment style was shaped by the way adults treated you when you lacked the power of choice, and this wounded attachment pattern may have made you susceptible to various challenges for which you likely blamed yourself. As a child, you adapted as best you could under the circumstances, demonstrating your resilience. You are a survivor. As an adult now, you can work with a therapist to reparent or retrain yourself to have a healthier attachment style for a happier future.

One of the biggest challenges faced after leaving the sex industry is dealing with the stigma and prejudice that will continue to follow you. In chapter 3, we explored the different ways to confront prejudice and embrace your self-worth. We discussed that stigma is not a reflection of who you are as a person and emphasized the importance of building a support system to help counteract negative attitudes.

Self-blame, shame, and guilt are common emotions experienced after leaving the sex industry. In chapter 4, we explored therapy, support groups, and self-reflection as strategies for emotional healing. We also discussed that emotions are a normal part of the healing process and self-compassion is an important part of moving forward.

Having a support system is crucial for anyone leaving the sex industry. In chapter 5, we explored different ways to build a support system, such as reaching out to family and friends, joining support groups, and seeking professional help. We also discussed what toxic relationships look like.

Unless you are already married, at some point you will likely want to date. Chapter 6, we discussed intimate relationships, how others will view you, the ramifications whether or not you disclose your past occupation, and how to disclose to a new partner if you have a permanent sexually transmitted infection.

There are toxic people who frequently target sex industry workers. In chapter 7, you learned about the different types of pimps and may have identified that you were indeed victimized by one. We also discussed stalkers and how you can protect yourself online and offline.

Finding a new career path or educational opportunity is an important part of moving forward in life. In chapter 8, we explored different options for career and education, vocational training, entrepreneurship, or returning to school. Numerous resources were provided. It was also highlighted that you find a career that you feel enthusiastic about and which is aligned with your interests and values. There is even a sample resume for those who have never done any other type of work.

Achieving financial independence is an essential part of moving forward in life after leaving the sex industry. Not only do you need it to survive, but you also need to be able to support yourself to maintain your own self-esteem. In chapter 9, we explored different strategies for personal finance and budgeting, such as creating a budget, reducing debt, and how to fix your credit.

Creating balance in life is new for many leaving the sex industry. In chapter 10, we explored different strategies for creating balance, such as setting boundaries, prioritizing self-care, and making new friends. We also discussed the importance of finding ways to integrate work, relationships, nutrition, and self-care into a healthy, fulfilling life.

Understanding legal rights and protections is important for everyone. In chapter 11, we explored different legal considerations, such as knowing your rights and finding legal assistance if necessary. We discussed the expungement and arrest relief process for those who want to clear up a past criminal record. Since family law is a common reason for going to court, that was also included.

Taking care of your physical and mental health is crucial during and after leaving the sex industry. In chapter 12, we explored different ways to prioritize physical and mental health, such as when you should seek psychiatric help and other alternatives. We also discussed body image, eating disorders, and finding ways to manage stress and build resilience.

Substance use is rampant in the adult industry. If you are quitting sex work yet realize that it is tough to stop partying, there is help. In Chapter 13, we detailed the differences between secular and Christian based 12-Step programs.

Chapter 14 is for the parents. Do you tell your children about your past? What if they find out on their or from friends? What if they were inappropriately exposed?

Trauma affects a great many sex workers due to trauma

before entering the industry and traumas related to work. In Chapter 15, we went over a comprehensive list of trauma treatments.

Chapter 16 was specifically about the sexual after-effects that those who have worked in the sex industry may experience. These are all common, yet rarely discussed. Two of them can potentially be a healthy lifestyle, whereas the other two are problematic.

For many individuals leaving the sex industry, spirituality and personal values are principal factors within their healing journey. In chapter 17, we explored different core beliefs, engaging in religious or spiritual practices, and exploring personal values. We also discussed the importance of identifying any misaligned beliefs you have adopted.

Maintaining progress over the long term is crucial for anyone leaving the sex industry. We explored different strategies for recognizing weaknesses, setting goals, tracking progress, and seeking continued support. We also discussed the importance of finding ways to celebrate successes and practice gratitude.

In conclusion, by leaving the sex industry you have begun a challenging journey of self-discovery and growth. While everyone's journey is unique, there are common themes and strategies that can be helpful for anyone seeking to move forward in their lives after leaving the sex industry. By embracing self-compassion and seeking support, you will be able to build a new life filled with purpose, meaning, and happiness. A holistic approach to healing and growth is key.

I hope that this book has prepared you with practical guidance, support, and new inspiration for your journey. It was my goal to create a single book that included much of what you would need in a one place and discuss many of the issues that are rarely discussed. When forewarned of issues you may face, it is easier to plan for success. And, if you are a survivor of exploitation and abuse, I hope that this book was validating for you and provided some healing words. This is a journey that requires patience, courage, and self-compassion. By reading this book, you now know what to expect and what it takes to succeed. With the right support, mindset, and tools, you will end up with a new fulfilling, joyful, and purposeful life. I encourage you to embrace your journey and believe in your potential and worth.

ABOUT THE AUTHOR

My story is not an uncommon one for a woman in the adult industry. For many years, I was under the control of a Romeo pimp, although I did not know the term. Manipulation is the most frequent method for pimping, and pimping through emotional and psychological manipulation is much more common than through physical threats or force. Having a pimp lowers your value and income potential, so many sex workers keep this secret. We are usually blamed for our own actions, and the pimps behind us are rarely outed or prosecuted. Most survivors are like me and believe they were at fault for what happened to them, so they never pursue legal recourse.

Before meeting that man, I was as part-time stripper. However, I was independent, all the money I earned went to me, and I would not do anything I was uncomfortable with. I had self-respect. After we started dating, he changed my stage name, told me what to say at work, how to act, what to do, and moved me to a different state far from my support network to maximize my earning potential. He drove me to and from work and held on to my money for me. He told me that these were acts of love, and I believed him.

A ton of sex workers become manipulated and controlled by articulate, well-educated, and "loving" pimps who did not fit the typical stereotype we had been warned to watch out for and even avoided. A pimp once said to me, *"If a pimp is doing his job right, the girl won't realize she is being pimped."* Sounds crazy, but true.

When I worked in Las Vegas, over 80% of the strippers I knew at top clubs had pimps. This was shocking to me, yet I had one too. When people think of pimps, they often imagine streetwalkers instead of strippers or high-end escorts. Anyone who is being forced or manipulated into sex work by someone else who profits in part or takes all of their earned money is being pimped—and this is frequently by their significant other.

I made a lot of money (at times up to $50k/month) yet rarely had money. When that ex and I broke up, I had nothing. He took almost everything while we were together, kept me stoned so I wouldn't notice or question it (I was sober before we got together), and took my savings when he left. He messed with my mental health, invaded my privacy, encouraged me to do things that kept me off balance, and hurt my self-esteem worse. He taught me that my appearance and sexuality were what defined my value. It took me years to unprogram that mindset.

Clearly, I have left much out of my story. For years, I self-medicated to cope with my inner shame. Eventually, I healed my wounds through extensive therapy. Yes, I participated in what happened. Not because I wanted that to be my life, but because I was manipulated into it...and that is what hurt the most. The first several times I said aloud what had happened, I could barely speak because I was crying so much.

That man continued to do things which hurt me for years afterward. However, now I am a strong woman, sober, and mentally stable. I no longer self-harm because there is no need; those secrets are no longer trapped inside and hurting me. I know I do not deserve punishment for who I used to be. Because I admitted to and accepted the reality of what I participated in and lived through, I have been able to forgive myself, forgive him, and move on with a healthy self-respect.

Through the grace of God, an organization for victims of human trafficking set me up with a therapist who understood these types of situations and she helped me to heal. Now I hold degrees in both psychology and counseling and work as a life coach so that I can give back by helping people who feel stuck. A decade ago, I never would have thought this was possible.

There was no guide to help me figure out how to quit the sex industry, heal myself, and start over in the mainstream world. Nobody warned me along the way about the continued judgment that does not end even after leaving sex work. It is my hope that this book will empower others to transition out of "the life" while simplifying their life-changing process. We are all worthy of love and happiness. Real love and happiness are not entangled with shame, pain, nor being controlled.

Your situation may or may not be similar to mine, yet either way you are reading this book to begin building a totally new life for yourself. The past is the past and you will never get that time back. However, your new life has the potential to be the best years of your life. Make that so. And... *congratulations!*

RESOURCES

1. The Sex Workers Project - Provides legal and social services for people who have worked in the sex industry. **https://sexworkersproject.org/**
2. The Sex Workers Outreach Project USA - National organization providing peer support, advocacy network for sex workers' rights, and resources for sex workers. **https://swopusa.org/**
3. The Cupcake Girls - Non-profit organization that provides support, resources, and empowerment for those in the adult industry. **https://www.thecupcakegirls.org/**
4. Portland Sex Worker Outreach Coalition - Promotes basic human rights and personal safety for all individuals working in the sex industry. **https://pdxswoc.wordpress.com/**
5. St. James Infirmary - Healthcare and support services for current and former sex workers in San Francisco, CA. **https://www.stjamesinfirmary.org/**
6. SWOP Sacramento - Peer support and advocacy for sex workers in Sacramento, CA. **https://sacramentoswop.org/**
7. Red Canary Song - Advocacy, language, legal, medical support for Asian migrant communities, sex working communities, and the overlap between the two. New York. **https://www.redcanarysong.net/**
8. Safe Horizon – Anti-trafficking, legal help, support groups, guidance, resources, and counseling. New York. **https://www.safehorizon.org/get-help/human-trafficking/**
9. Legal Aid Society - Legal services for people who have worked in the sex industry in New York City. **https://legalaidnyc.org/programs-projects-units/exploitation-intervention-project/**
10. The Urban Justice Center - Legal services for sex workers and trafficking survivors in New York City. **https://swp.urbanjustice.org/**

11. Project Legacy - No-cost supportive services such as case management and referrals, peer support groups, individual therapy, rental assistance, basic needs, vocational and college tuition assistance, educational resources, and credit counseling. Minnesota. **https://projectlegacymn.org/**
12. Lysistrata Mutual Care Collective - A mutual aid group for sex workers in Austin, TX. **https://www.lysistratamccf.org/**
13. The Empowerment Program - Job training, education, and support for those who have experienced poverty, homelessness, or sex trafficking. **https://www.empowermentprogram.org/**
14. SWOP Behind Bars - Support and resources for incarcerated people who have worked in the sex industry. **https://www.swopbehindbars.org/**
15. Sista II Sista - Support and advocacy for women of color who have worked in the sex industry. Memphis, TN. **https://www.sista2sista.co/**
16. SWAN Vancouver - Peer support and advocacy for sex workers in Vancouver, Canada. **https://swanvancouver.ca/**
17. The Butterfly Asian and Migrant Sex Workers – Support, resources, and education for people leaving the sex industry. Toronto, Canada. **https://www.butterflysw.org/**
18. Maggie's Toronto. **https://www.maggiesto.org/**
19. Sex Workers' Action Program Hamilton – Supplies for safer sex, Naloxone/Narcan kits, mental health, housing, childcare, clothing, and food resources, curated occupational health and safety protocols, personal advocacy, interactive workshops, and public awareness campaigns. Ontario, Canada. **https://swaphamilton.com/**
20. The Justice Project - Comprehensive knowledge of the intersection of irregular migration, sexual violence, prostitution, and human trafficking within central Europe and counselling, accompaniment, advocacy, and support to

women who have been trafficked for the purpose of sexual exploitation. **https://www.thejusticeproject.net/**
21. The Red Project - Practical advice and emotional support for sex workers affected by, or at risk of, sexual violence in the UK. **https://theredproject.co.uk/**
22. Survivors' Network - Provides support and advocacy for people who have experienced sexual violence, including those who have worked in the sex industry. United Kingdom. **https://survivorsnetwork.org.uk/**
23. Women's Support Project - A Scottish organization that provides support and advocacy for women who have experienced violence or abuse, including those who have worked in the sex industry. **https://www.womenssupportproject.org.uk/**
24. Sex Workers Alliance Ireland - Peer support and advocacy for sex workers in Ireland. **https://sexworkersallianceireland.org/**
25. Decriminalize Sex Work - A global network of organizations advocating for the decriminalization of sex work. **https://decriminalizesex.work/**
26. Global Network of Sex Work Project (NSWP) - Advocates for rights-based services, freedom from abuse and discrimination, freedom from punitive laws, policies and practices, and self-determination for sex workers. **https://www.nswp.org/**
27. European Sex Workers Rights Alliance - Advocacy group working towards the recognition and protection of sex workers' human rights. **https://www.eswalliance.org/**

Help when being stalked
- National Domestic Violence Hotline: 1-800-799-SAFE

(7233). Offers 24/7 support to victims of domestic violence, which can include stalking. Trained advocates are available to provide confidential support, resources, and referrals to local services. **https://www.thehotline.org/**
- Cyber Civil Rights Initiative (CCRI): 1-844-878-2274. CCRI focuses on online harassment and nonconsensual pornography (also known as "revenge porn"). They offer a crisis helpline, resources for victims, and advocacy to raise awareness and promote legal reform. **https://www.cybercivilrights.org/**
- Love is Respect: 1-866-331-9474, text "LOVEIS" to 22522 Provides support, resources, and advocacy for young people affected by dating violence, including stalking. They offer a 24/7 helpline, online chat, and text support. **https://www.loveisrespect.org/**
- Without My Consent: Aims to combat online harassment, especially nonconsensual distribution of intimate images and online impersonation. They provide resources for victims and educational materials to promote awareness and understanding of the issues. **https://www.withoutmyconsent.org/**
- Working to Halt Online Abuse (WHOA): A volunteer organization dedicated to helping victims of online harassment and cyberstalking. They provide resources, assistance, and advice for dealing with various forms of online abuse. **https://www.haltabuse.org/**

Non-occupational crisis help
SAMHSA (Substance Abuse and Mental Health Services Administration): call 1-800-662-HELP (4357) or online at **https://www.samhsa.gov/find-help**
RAINN (Rape, Abuse & Incest National Network): 1-800-656-HOPE (4673) or online at **https://www.rainn.org/**
Rape Crisis England & Wales - 0808 500 222 or online at **https://rapecrisis.org.uk/get-help/want-to-talk/**

To protect your privacy
ExpressVPN – **https://www.expressvpn.com/**
Private Internet Access VPN – **https://privateinternetaccess.com/**
CyberGhost VPN – **https://www.cyberghostvpn.com/**
Torguard VPN – **https://torguard.net/**
NordVPN – **https://nordvpn.com/**
Mic-Lock (for your cell phone and computer) – **https://mic-lock.com/**

Books I recommend
Complex PTSD – Pete Walker
The Body Keeps the Score – Bessel van Der Kolk
The Gift of Fear – Gavin deBruin
You Can Survive Narcissist Abuse – Melanie Tonia Evans
Act Like a Lady, Think Like a Man – Steve Harvey
The Father Daughter Talk – RC Blakes Jr.
The Betrayal Bond – Patrick Carnes

www.ingramcontent.com/pod-product-compliance
Lightning Source LLC
Chambersburg PA
CBHW060514090426
42735CB00011B/2216